Books in this inspirational series
distributed by Doubleday & Company, Inc.

Dreams, books, are each a world;
   and books, we know,
      Are a substantial world,
         both pure and good.
            Round these, with tendrils strong
               as flesh and blood,
                  Our pastime and our happiness
                     will grow.

—WILLIAM WORDSWORTH
From *Personal Talk, Sonnet 3*

Presenting . . .

TREASURED
THOUGHTS

TREASURED THOUGHTS

Selections from many sources
providing
reading for casual enjoyment
thoughts for patient perusal
and
nonsense for pleasant pastime

Edited by
Thomas C. Jones

J. G. FERGUSON PUBLISHING COMPANY
CHICAGO

DISTRIBUTED TO THE BOOK TRADE BY DOUBLEDAY & COMPANY, INC.

COMMENT BY THE EDITOR,
AND ACKNOWLEDGMENTS

As we enter the last third of the twentieth century, the complications of just plain living frequently seem to be overwhelming. The body can absorb amazing pressures without destroying the spirit. Man has an infinite capacity to adjust to the problems of the day. Yet, for many, our total culture is changing too rapidly to permit this marvelous physical machine to function at its normal efficiency. It becomes more and more difficult to close out the events of the day from our lives because of the ubiquitous world of electronics and communications.

Treasured Thoughts may help to provide fifteen minutes or perhaps an hour's surcease from the cares and confusions of daily living. The entries are divided into six categories that loosely fit the subject matter of the writing. There are one hundred and fifty selections — poems, quotations, essays, and stories — in this collection. The sources vary from *The Holy Bible* to *Spink's Sports Stories*, and from *Epictetus* to *Edward Lear*.

Unlike the conventional anthology, which typically is restricted to a single form of literary expression by prestigious authors, the range, style, form, subject matter, or prestige of the author has nothing to do with the contents of this volume. These selections were made on the basis of their interest value, inspirational or humorous appeal, historical relations to the conditions of the day, or just plain good reading for the weary soul who would rather be surprised and (we hope) pleased with some little obscure gem from the past than to know that on the next page there is a poem by Keats. Not that we eschew Keats, for he is represented in this book, but the purpose here is to provide a continuous change of style and subject.

We have separate sections for the ladies and the men, but this does not mean that they are mutually exclusive. *A Christmas Wish* by Eugene Field, *Our Kind of a Man* by James Whitcomb Riley, *Qualities of a Friend* by William Penn, and *Concerning Friendship* by Cicero are all entries that will appeal to men, although they have been selected for *Of Special Interest to the Ladies*. Likewise, there are entries in *Mostly for Men* that will appeal to women, such as *The Urgency of Better Education* by John F. Kennedy, *The Spirit of America* by Woodrow Wilson, and *Solitude* by Lewis Carroll.

Some of the articles that seem to have particular pertinence to the issues of the day are *The Myth of the Communist Superman* by Clarence B. Randall, *Post Office Problems Before the Zip Code* by Marshall Cushing, *Give Some Meaning to Education* by John Dewey, *After the Election the President Represents All the People* by Alfred E. Smith, *What Is True Patriotism?* by Sydney J. Harris, *Dissidents in His Own Party Wanted to Defeat Lincoln in 1864* by Carl Schurz, *Every Generation Has Been Plagued by Taxes, Class of '68 as Seen by '18* by John S. Knight, *There Is a Better Weapon than the H-Bomb* by John F. Kennedy, and *Those Who Encourage Anarchy at Home Join Hands with Our Enemies Abroad* by Theodore Roosevelt.

Every male reader will be fascinated by *Dempsey versus Carpentier*, the story of the heavyweight championship bout that thrilled the nation nearly fifty years ago. The vivid description by Al Spink makes the action as real as if it were being viewed on the latest color television. The business man will suffer with Noah Webster in the narration of his traumatic experiences in *Disappointments in Producing America's First Dictionary*. Since this is a political year, there are those who will enjoy *Naming the Republican Party* by C. A. Church, and almost everyone will chuckle at *Jack Gay Abroad and at Home, or The Party Boy Unmasked* by Laman Blanchard.

No collection such as this is attractive to the reader without care, design, and artistry. We have been most fortunate in the devotion to the finished product shown by qualified persons in all categories. To my assistant, Harriet Helmer, I must acknowledge an enthusiastic and talented spirit without which this would be a much diminished effort. The art by Kay Lovelace Smith is both appealing and appropriate. General layout and design by Al Josephson of Photopress, Inc., and dedication to the finest in the Graphic Arts by the entire Photopress organization have contributed greatly to whatever distinction can be attached to this volume. The A. C. Engdahl bindery and certainly the A-1 Composition Company have both helped tremendously in bringing out a worthy volume. Finally, the Creative and Sales Departments of Brown and Bigelow, St. Paul, Minnesota, have been the inspiration to guide us.

We have drawn upon many sources and must express sincere appreciation to both publishers and authors for their courteous and prompt response to our requests for permissions. We take pleasure in acknowledging below the publishers and authors to whom we are indebted:

American Mercury, Box 1306, Torrance, California 90505 —*What Is a Statesman?* by Charles A. Beard, from *The American Mercury*, April, 1924. Atlantic-Little, Brown and Company — *The Myth of the Communist Superman*, from *The Folklore of Management*, copyright © 1959, 1960, 1961, by Clarence B. Randall. Chicago Daily News — *A Rare Horoscope for the Followers of the Stars* by Mike Royko. Reprinted with permission from the *Chicago Daily News*, from Mike Royko's column. Dodd, Mead and Company, Inc. — *Song, Thoughts on the Shape of the Human Body, The Way That Lovers Use*, and *The Wayfarers*, from *The Collected Poems of Rupert Brooke*. Copyright

Waldo Emerson. *American History by American Poets*, edited by Nellie Urner Wallington. Copyright 1911, by Duffield & Company. *The American Remembrancer, or an Impartial Collection of Essays, Resolves, Speeches, etc. Relative to the Treaty with Great Britain.* A. S. Barnes & Company — *The Magazine of American History.* Belford, Clarke & Company — *Poems of Passion* by Ella Wheeler Wilcox. Bell and Daldy, London — *George Cruikshank's Table-Book* edited by Gilbert Abbott a Beckett. The Bibliophile Society — *Love Letters of James Whitcomb Riley.* Copyright, 1922, by the Bibliophile Society. William Blackwood and Sons, Edinburgh — *Songs and Poems* by Thomas Tod Stoddart. Brockwell Company, Cincinnati — *Old Wagon Show Days* by Gil Robinson. Robert John Bush, London — *Laughable Lyrics* by Edward Lear. H. M. Caldwell Company — *Discourses of Epictetus.* *Campaign Addresses of Governor Alfred E. Smith,* issued by The Democratic National Committee, Washington. Copyright 1929 by Alfred E. Smith. *Camp-Fire Chats of the Civil War* by Washington Davis. *George Cruikshank's Omnibus. The Cynic's Word Book* by Ambrose Bierce. Copyright, 1906, by Doubleday, Page & Company. *A Discourse on Old Age* by Marcus Tullius Cicero, translated by Benjamin Franklin. M. A. Donohue & Company — *The Life and Sayings of Theodore Roosevelt* by Thomas Handford. *The Florentine Fior di Virtu of 1491,* translated by Nicholas Fersin, published for the Library of Congress — 1953. Glazier & Company — *The Federalist, on the New Constitution,* written in 1788 by Mr. Hamilton, Mr. Madison, and Mr. Jay. *History of the Republican Party in Illinois* by C. A. Church. Copyright 1912 by C. A. Church. Houghton, Mifflin and Company — *Abraham Lincoln* by Carl Schurz. *The Spirit of Montaigne* edited by Grace Norton, copyright 1908 by Grace Norton. Hurst and Blackett, London—*The Wabash: or Adventures of an English Gentleman's Family in the Interior of America,* by J. Richard Beste. King James Version of *The Holy Bible. The Life of Andrew Jackson* by John Spencer Bassett, copyright 1911 by Doubleday, Page & Company. *Life of the Honorable Thomas McKean, LL.D.* by Roberdeau Buchanan. Longmans, Green, and Company, London — *Old-Fashioned Roses* by James Whitcomb Riley. *McGuffey's New Third Eclectic Reader,* 1857. Meador Publishing Company, Boston — *The Story of Concord,* copyright 1939 by Josephine Latham Swayne. *Notes on the Life of Noah Webster,* compiled by Emily Ellsworth Fowler Ford. William Pickering, London — *History of Letter-Writing* by William Roberts. Pocket Books, Inc. — *Franklin Delano Roosevelt, A Memorial,* edited by Donald Porter Geddes. Copyright, 1945, by Pocket Books, Inc. William Reynolds, Daniel Griffin, New York — *The Pride of Britannia Humbled* by William Cobbett. B. B. Russell & Company, Boston — *The History of Maine* by John S. C. Abbott. Scott-Thaw Company — *Some Fruits of Solitude* by William Penn. Simms and McIntyre, London — *A Stroll Through the Diggings of California* by William Kelly. Tandy, Wheeler & Company — *A Little Book of Tribune Verse* by Eugene Field. A. M. Thayer & Company — *The Story of Our Post Office* by Marshall Cushing. Raphael Tuck and Sons Company, Limited — *The Year Book of American Authors* written and edited by Ida Scott Taylor. The University of Chicago Press — *The School and Society,* copyright 1900 by John Dewey. Weidenfeld and Nicolson, London — *A History of Western Morals* © 1959 by Crane Brinton. Wentworth & Company — *The Christian Counsellor; or Jewels for the Household* edited by Tryon Edwards. Wiggin & Lunt — *Plain Dealing* by Thomas Lechford. *Wit and Wisdom of Woodrow Wilson,* compiled and classified by Richard Linthicum. Copyright, 1916, by Doubleday, Page & Company.

TABLE OF CONTENTS

Fact and Fable—Prose and Poetry

TABLE OF CONTENTS

Glimpses of the American Past

Of Special Interest to the Ladies

Bits of Fun

TABLE OF CONTENTS

Items of Unusual Interest

Mostly for Men

Fact and Fable

❖

Prose and Poetry

Two Interpretations of the Happy Life

A sixteenth-century version by Henry Howard, Earl of Surrey

Martial, the things for to attain
The happy life be these, I find:
The riches left, not got with pain;
The fruitful ground; the quiet mind;
The equal friend; no grudge, nor strife;
No charge of rule nor governance;
Without disease, the healthful life;
The household of continuance;
The mean diet, no delicate fare;
Wisdom joined with simplicity;
The night discharged of all care,
Where wine may bear no sovereignty;
The chaste wife, wise, without debate;
Such sleeps as may beguile the night;
Contented with thine own estate,
Neither wish death, nor fear his might.

Martial, Book X, No. 47

A twentieth-century version by Gilbert Highet

To bring yourself to be happy
Acquire the following blessings:
A nice inherited income,
A kindly farm with a kitchen,
No business worries or lawsuits,
Good health, a gentleman's muscles,
A wise simplicity, friendships,
A plain but generous table,
Your evenings sober but jolly,
Your bed amusing but modest,
And nights that pass in a moment;
To be yourself without envy,
To fear not death, nor to wish it.

Martial, Book X, No. 47

Homespun Philosophy

An early start makes easy stages.

I'd rather keep a creature whose faults I do know than change him for a beast whose faults I don't know.

Politics makes a man as crooked as a pack does a peddler— not that they are so awfully heavy, but it *teaches a man to stoop* in the long run.

We can do without any article of luxury we've never had, but when once obtained, it is not in human nature to surrender it voluntarily.

If a man doesn't hoe his corn and he doesn't get a crop, he says it's all owing to the bank; and if he runs into debt and is sued, why, he says the lawyers are a curse to the country.

Society is something like a barrel of pork. The meat that's at the top is sometimes not as good as that that's a little grain lower down; the upper and lower ends are troublesomely apt to have a little taint in them, but the middle is always good.

You may differ as much as you please about the style of a young lady's figure, but I tell you confidentially, if she has $100,000, the figure is about as near right as you will get it.

The man is not always a thief who steals a march.

Honesty is like an icicle. If it once melts that's the last of it.

When a man dies the first thing we talk about is his wealth, the next thing his failings, and the last thing his virtues.

It is true that wealth won't make a man virtuous, but I notice there isn't anyone who wants to be poor just for the purpose of being good.

Be Willing To Take Advice

An observation by Benjamin Franklin

Benjamin Franklin once received a very useful lesson from Dr. Cotton Mather, noted minister of the Old North Church in Boston, which he thus related in a letter to Dr. Mather's son:

"The last time I saw your father was in 1724. On taking my leave, he showed me a shorter way out of the house, by a narrow passage which was crossed by a beam overhead. We were still talking as I withdrew, he accompanying me behind, and I turning toward him, when he said hastily, 'Stoop, stoop!' I did not understand him till I felt my head hit against the beam.

"Dr. Mather was a man who never missed an opportunity of giving instruction, and upon this he said to me, 'You are young, and have the world before you; learn to stoop as you go through it, and you will avoid many hard thumps.'

"This advice, thus beat into my head, has frequently been of use to me; and I often think of it when I see pride mortified and misfortune brought upon people by their carrying their heads too high."

First Prayer in Congress

A report, with an excerpt from a letter
by John Adams to his wife

When Congress first met, Thomas Cushing of Boston, son of a wealthy merchant, moved that it should be opened with prayer. This was opposed on the ground that the members, being of various denominations, were so divided in their religious sentiments that they could not join in any one mode of worship. Mr. Samuel Adams arose, and after saying he was no bigot, and could hear a prayer from any gentleman of piety and virtue who was a friend to his country, moved that Rev. Mr. Duché—an Episcopal clergyman, who, he said, he understood deserved that character—be invited to read prayers before

Congress the next morning. The motion was passed; and the next morning Mr. Duché appeared, and after reading several prayers in the established form, then read the collect for the 7th of September, which was the thirty-fifth psalm.

This was the next morning after the startling news had come of the cannonade of Boston; and says John Adams, "I never saw a greater effect upon an audience: it seemed as if Heaven had ordained that psalm to be read on that morning." "After this," he continues, "Mr. Duché, unexpectedly to everybody, struck out into an extemporaneous prayer, which filled the bosom of every man present. I never heard a better prayer, or one so well pronounced. Dr. Cooper himself never prayed with such fervor, ardor, earnestness, and pathos, and in language so eloquent and sublime, for America, for the Congress, for the province of Massachusetts bay, and especially for Boston. It had an excellent effect upon everybody here;" and many, he tells us, were melted to tears.

✶

A Psalm of David

Plead my cause, O Lord, with them that strive with me; fight against them that fight against me.

Take hold of shield and buckler, and stand up for mine help.

Draw out also the spear, and stop the way against them that persecute me: say unto my soul, I am thy salvation.

Let them be confounded and put to shame that seek after my soul: let them be turned back and brought to confusion that devise my hurt.

Let them be as chaff before the wind: and let the angel of the Lord chase them.

Let their way be dark and slippery: and let the angel of the Lord persecute them.

For without cause have they hid for me their net in a pit, which without cause they have digged for my soul.

Let destruction come upon him at unawares; and let his net that he hath hid catch himself: into that very destruction let him fall.

PSALMS 35:1–8

Why Fear Old Age?

Written about 52 B.C. by MARCUS TULLIUS CICERO

It is alleged that memory fails in old age. That it does so, I freely grant; but then it is principally, where it has not been properly exercised; or with those who naturally have no strength of brain: for such as have, will pretty well retain it. Themistocles could call every citizen of Athens by his name; and do you think, when he became old, that if he met Aristides, he would salute him by the name of Lysimachus? For my own part, I not only know those who are now living, but I remember their fathers and grandfathers: nor when I read over the inscriptions of the tombs, do I find I am in danger of losing mine.

I never yet heard of an old man that forgot where he had hid his treasure. The oldest will remember what engages their thoughts and care, as when they give or take security, with such other affairs as concern them. How do the lawyers, the pontiffs, the augurs, and the philosophers, who live to a great age? What a vast number of particulars must all these comprehend in their memories? Men will retain their understanding and abilities, while they continue their application and diligence. This we find true, not only in men of great and public characters, but in those also, who have lived a quiet and inactive life, and spent it only in study. Sophocles wrote tragedies at a very great age, and when his sons, apprehending that through his application to that business alone, he neglected all his other affairs, and consequently they would be ruined; they cited him into court, that (as you know it is with us, when people by their ill conduct ruin their estate, it is taken from them, and committed to better hands; so) the judges of Athens should take the same order with him, as with those who become incapable of business.

He is said to have read to the judges a part of his tragedy, called Oedipus Coloneus, that he had then in hand, and to have asked them, whether they thought that the work of a dotard? upon which they acquitted him. Consider then, whether age can be truly said to destroy the capacity, or extinguish the abilities of the mind.

"Beauty Is in the Eye of the Beholder"

by IDA SCOTT TAYLOR

Cultivate a taste for the beautiful. Train your eye to distinguish the lovely harmonies in nature; get into the spirit of the season, whatever it is, and always find something worth seeing and remembering. Surely God never meant that any of His wonders should be overlooked; the smallest flower that blossoms, the tiniest seed that sprouts, is His handiwork. The more you study His creations, the nearer you should be drawn to Him. No matter what your calling is, get as near to the heart of God as you can through it. If He has given you an artist's soul, how thankful you should be; then you are indeed blest, because you can be a blessing to others. If you can put on canvas a reflection of earth's loveliness, you have been chosen by your Heavenly Father to do a special work for Him by using your gift for His glory.

Though we travel the world over to find the beautiful, we must carry it with us, or we find it not. The best of beauty is a finer charm than skill in surfaces, in outlines, or rules of art can ever teach; namely, a radiation from the work of art of human character.

—RALPH WALDO EMERSON

Special Qualities of the Wise Man

by WILLIAM PENN

The *Wise* Man Governs himself by the *Reason* of his Case, and because what he does is *Best*: Best, in a Moral and Prudent, not a *Sinister* Sense.

He proposes just Ends, and employs the *fairest* and most probable Means and Methods to attain them.

Though you cannot always penetrate his Design, or his Reasons for it, yet you shall ever see his Actions of a *Piece*, and his Performances like a *Workman*: They will bear the *Touch* of Wisdom and Honor, as often as they are tried.

He scorns to serve himself by *Indirect Means*, or be an *Interloper* in Government, since just Enterprises never want any Just *Ways* to succeed them.

To do Evil, that Good may come of it, is for *Bunglers* in Politics, as well as Morals.

Like those Surgeons, that will cut off an Arm they can't cure, to *hide* their Ignorance and save their Credit.

The *Wise* Man is *Cautious*, but not cunning; *Judicious*, but not crafty; making Virtue the *Measure* of using his Excellent Understanding in the Conduct of his Life.

The *Wise* Man is equal, ready, but not *officious*; has in every Thing an Eye to *Sure Footing*. He offends nobody, nor *easily* is offended, and always willing to Compound for *Wrongs*, if not forgive them.

He is never Captious, nor Critical; hates *Banter* and *Jests*. He may be Pleasant, but not Light; he never deals but in *Substantial Ware*, and leaves the rest for the *Toy Pates* (or Shops) of the *World*; which are so far from being his Business, that they are not so much as his *Diversion*.

He is always for some solid Good, *Civil* or *Moral*; as, to make his Country more *Virtuous*, Preserve her Peace and Liberty, Employ her Poor, Improve Land, Advance Trade, Suppress Vice, Encourage Industry, and all Mechanic Knowledge; and that they should be the *Care* of the Government, and the Blessing and Praise of the People.

To conclude: He is Just, and *fears God, hates Covetousness and eschews Evil, and loves his Neighbor as himself.*

"Difficulties are the things that show what men are"

Written about 90 A.D. by Epictetus

Difficulties are the things that show what men are. For the future, on any difficulty, remember that God, like an instructor of athletics, has engaged you with a rough antagonist.

For what end?

That you may be a conqueror like one in the Olympic games, and it cannot be without toil. No man, in my opinion, has a more advantageous difficulty on his hands than you have; provided you will but use it as an athletic champion doth his antagonist. We are now sending a spy to Rome; but no one ever sends a timorous spy, who, when he only hears a noise or sees a shadow, runs back, frightened out of his wits, and says: "The enemy is just at hand." So now, if you should come and tell us: "Things are in a fearful way at Rome, death is terrible; banishment, terrible; calumny, terrible; poverty, terrible; run, good people, the enemy is at head:" we will answer: Get you gone, and prophesy for yourself; our only fault is that we have sent such a spy.

Diogenes was sent a spy before you; but he told us other tidings. He says that death is no evil, for it is nothing base; that defamation is only the noise of madmen. And what account did this spy give us of pain? Of pleasure? Of poverty? He says that to be naked is better than a purple robe, to sleep upon the bare ground the softest bed, and gives a proof of all he says by his own courage, tranquillity, and freedom; and, moreover, by a healthy and robust body. There is no enemy near, says he. All is profound peace.—How so, Diogenes? Look upon me, says he. Am I hurt? Am I wounded? Have I run away from any one? This is such a spy as he ought to be. But you come and tell us one thing after another. Go back again and examine things more exactly and without fear.

Who looking backward from his manhood's prime,
Sees not the spectre of his misspent time?

—JOHN GREENLEAF WHITTIER

The Calendar of Life

Hark to the squalling newborn Year!
  Squalling with wind, and crying with sleet;
Old Dame January is here,
    With snow-white cap, and slippers on feet:
      She is his nurse, and she hugs him, rocks him,
      And into blankets she cuddles him, tucks him—
    Then sips something so strong and so sweet!

Now to school—in the biting air—
  Much to shiver, little to learn—
February in state sits there,
    Frosty old Pedagogue, sharp and stern:
      In cold corner he claps him, taps him,
      And over the knuckles he raps him, slaps him,
    Once and again till his fingers burn.

Then a shipboy—ready of hand,
  Sturdy of heart, though the sea be rough;
Commodore March is there in command,
    Stout Sea-Captain, stormy and bluff;
      Noisily ever he rates him, trains him—
      Storm or shipwreck awaits him, drains him—
    But his heart is fresh, and his nerves are tough.

Just as the pigeons begin to pair,
  He feels a pleasure, and calls it pain;
Young Lady April fickle and fair,
    Rules his heart with a fitful reign;
      Now she is frowning, and beckons him, moves him—
      Now she avows that she likes him, loves him,
    Darting a smile through the clouds again.

But soon hawking at higher game—
  Shadow for substance passing away—
Now the queen of his heart is Fame—
    Life in its vigour and prime, and May:
      She has flowers to tease him, grace him,
      And sharp lessons to teach him, brace him—
    Like shrewd winds on a sunny day.

Now he thrills with a fierce delight;
Prancing past in his pomp appears
Captain 𝕵une, with his streamers bright—
Flashing, thundering, flanked with fears;
War is the cry, and he takes him, arms him—
Proud is the pageant, and dazzles him, charms him,
But flashes are followed by floods—of tears.

Calmly and brightly shines the sun—
Ripens his heart, with the golden grain—
Sweet 𝕵uly he has wooed and won—
Doubled his pleasure, halved his pain:
Her sunny smile ever helps him, lights him—
Though, as her faith she trusts him, plights him,
She shed some drops of a gentle rain.

But when the scythe and the sickle come,
Comes a new comfort with a new care:
Fruitful 𝕬ugust has blest his home—
Crowned are his hopes with an infant heir:
Tears and smiles follow, to push him, please him—
Work and play now do rush him, seize him,
Filling the father's heart with cheer.

Fortune now is his idol grown—
Houses, and lands, and worldly ware—
Life's 𝕾eptember has come and gone,
Fickle as April—seldom so fair;
Riches and rank may be with him, near him—
Sport and good claret may warm him, cheer him,
But where are the joys of his youth—ah where?

Soon enters change to play its part—
Nature doffs her colors at the call;
Golden 𝕺ctober has breathed on his heart,
Searing over the green spots all:
Ties are breaking that helped him, bound him—
Friends are falling near him, around him,
Just as the leaves in the Autumn fall.

Now, he sits, and snores in his chair—
   Feet to the fire—wrapped in gown so sleek:
Rugged 𝔑𝔬𝔳𝔢𝔪𝔟𝔢𝔯 is suddenly there.
   Feeling his pulse—slower and weak:
      Night and morning no longer divide—
      The pleasures are simple and all coincide,
And December arrives, cold and bleak.

Clattering hoofs on the hard ground ring:
   What rider dismounts in garb so fine?
'Tis 𝔇𝔢𝔠𝔢𝔪𝔟𝔢𝔯, the winter king—
   'Tis King Christmas, with a flagon of wine!
      Draped in tinsel and frost, he smiles as he meets him—
      Lively and laughing, he shouts as he greets him—
Good cheer to you all! Happy Sixty-nine!

Ambition Is a Fearful Ship

by WASHINGTON DAVIS

Ambition is a fearful ship to fight with;
It tosses man's imagination up
To the shaky pinnacle of its desires;
Then lets him fall a flat, insipid thing,
With only lax, low spirits in his frame.
It takes away his sleep; it both consumes
And quickens youthful hearts, which thus grow good,
Then great.
          But still Ambition yields at times,
And in that weakness is God-given; for,
When Judgment's captain, and Obedience
The helmsman, then Ambition is compelled
To take that safe, though unsailed stream which flows
In triumph through the ocean of the world—
Clear of the rocks and reefs of circumstance.
Then, with a virtuous, well-trained crew,
She may at will seek her desired harbor.

Postal Rates Are Down!

by WILLIAM H. WALLACE

From *The Story of Our Post Office* by MARSHALL CUSHING

Yes, this is true compared to the rates in 1835, as you will see in this summary of charges.

Old time rates of postage were figured thus:

For a single letter carried 30 miles	6¼¢ (called then a fip)
Thence up to 80 miles	10¢
Thence up to 150 miles	12½¢ eleven pence)
Thence up to 400 miles	18¾¢ (three fips)
400 miles or to any part of the United States	25¢

Storekeepers in those early days were in the habit of taking all kinds of country or farm trade for goods, and where a post office was connected with the store, it was as common to take produce for letters and papers as for goods.

The prices of produce varied some seasons, but butter and eggs were always low in summer, the prevailing price being 6¼ cents a pound for the former and 5 cents per dozen for the latter.

To illustrate: To pay postage on a 25-cent letter it required the amount of the following articles separately:

4 pounds of butter
5 dozen eggs
2 bushels of oats
2 bushels of potatoes
1⅓ pounds of common, coarse wool
A little over ⅔ of a bushel of wheat
Other articles in proportion

To illustrate further the cost of the expense of correspondence: Suppose a farmer and family communicated with a New York correspondent and had to receive 32 unpaid letters. He must sell a good milch cow to foot the postage bill, for $8 would buy a good cow. It made it obligatory upon the postmaster, as far as it was possible, to scrutinize rigidly every letter—and if it consisted of two pieces of paper, then double postage was charged.

by E<small>UGENE</small> F<small>IELD</small>

I am an advertiser great!
    In letters bold
    The praises of my wares I sound,
Prosperity is my estate;
    The people come,
    The people go
    In one continuous,
    Surging flow.
They buy my goods and come again
And I'm the happiest of men;
And this the reason I relate,
I'm an advertiser great!

There is a shop across the way
    Where ne'er is heard a human tread,
    Where trade is paralyzed and dead,
With ne'er a customer a day.
    The people come,
    The people go,
    But never there.
    They do not know
There's such a shop beneath the skies,
Because *he* does not advertise!
While I with pleasure contemplate
That I'm an advertiser great.

The secret of my fortune lies
   In one small fact, which I may state,
   Too many tradesmen learn too late,
If I have goods, I advertise.
   Then people come
   And people go
   In constant streams,
   For people know
That he who has good wares to sell
Will surely advertise them well;
And proudly I reiterate,
I am an advertiser great!

The Seven Sticks

From *McGuffey's New Third Eclectic Reader—1857*

A man had seven sons, who were always quarreling. They left their studies and work, to quarrel among themselves.

Some bad men were looking forward to the death of their father, to cheat them out of their property, by making them quarrel about it.

The good old man, one day, called his sons around him.

He laid before them seven sticks, which were bound together. He said, "I will pay a hundred dollars to the one who can break this bundle."

Each one strained every nerve to break the bundle. After a long, but vain trial, they all said that it could not be done.

"And yet," said the father, "nothing is easier." He then untied the bundle, and broke the sticks, one by one, with perfect ease.

"Ah!" said his sons, "it is easy enough to do it so; any body could do it in that way."

Their father replied, "As it is with these sticks, so is it with you, my sons. So long as you hold fast together, you will prosper, and none can injure you.

"But if the bond of union be broken, it will happen to you as to these sticks, which lie here, broken, on the ground."

Truisms

I cannot but often wonder to see fathers who love their sons very well yet so order the matter by a constant stiffness and a mien of authority and distance to them all their lives, as if they were never to enjoy or have any comfort from those they love best in the world, till they have lost them by being removed into another.

* * * * *

Be sure not to let your son be bred up in the art and formality of disputing ... questioning everything, and thinking there is no such thing as truth to be sought, but only victory, in disputing.

* * * * *

Children are often found to tread too near upon the heels of their fathers, to the no great satisfaction either of son or father.

* * * * *

Children may be taught to read, without perceiving it to be anything but a sport, and play themselves into that which others are whipped for.

* * * * *

I imagine you would think him a very foolish fellow that should not value a virtuous or a wise man, infinitely before a great scholar. Not but that I think learning a great help to both in well-disposed minds. ... [But] when you are looking out for a schoolmaster or a tutor [for your son] you would not have Latin and logic ... only in your thoughts. Learning must be had but in the second place, as subservient only to greater qualities. Seek out somebody that may know how discreetly to frame his manners.

From *Some Thoughts Concerning Education* by John Locke

As for the knowing of men which is at second hand from reports; men's weaknesses and faults are best known from their enemies, their virtues and abilities from their friends, their customs and times from their servants, their conceits and opinions from their familiar friends with whom they converse most. General fame is light, and the opinions conceived by superiors or equals are deceitful, for to such, men are more masked.

From *The Advancement of Learning* by Francis Bacon

* * * * *

He Knew as Much as I

by JOHN MARSTON

I was a scholar: seven useful springs
Did I deflower in quotations
Of cross'd opinions 'bout the soul of man;
The more I learnt, the more I learnt to doubt.
Delight, my spaniel, slept, whilst I baused leaves,
Toss'd o'er the dunces, pored on the old print
Of titled words; and still my spaniel slept.

Still on went I; first, *an sit anima;*
Then, an it were mortal. O hold! hold! at that
They're at brain buffets, fell by the ears amain
Pell-mell together; still my spaniel slept.
Then whether 't were corporeal, local, fix'd,
Ex traduce, but whether 't had free will
Or no, hot philosophers
Stood banding factions, all so strongly propp'd,
I stagger'd, knew not which was firmer part,
But thought, quoted, read, observ'd and pry'd,
Stuff'd noting-books; and still my spaniel slept.
At length he waked and yawn'd; and by yon sky,
For aught I know, he knew as much as I.

From *What You Will*—1607

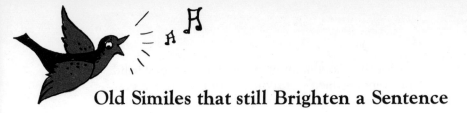

Old Similes that still Brighten a Sentence

As wet as a fish—as dry as a bone;
As live as a bird—as dead as a stone;
As plump as a partridge—as poor as a rat;
As strong as a horse—as weak as a cat;
As hard as a flint—as soft as a mole;
As white as a lily—as black as a coal;
As plain as a pike-staff—as rough as a bear;
As light as a drum—as free as the air;
As heavy as lead—as light as a feather;
As steady as time—uncertain as weather;
As hot as an oven—as cold as a frog;
As gay as a lark—as sick as a dog;
As slow as the tortoise—as swift as the wind;
As true as the Gospel—as false as mankind;
As thin as a herring—as fat as a pig;
As proud as a peacock—as blithe as a grig;
As savage as tigers—as mild as a dove;
As stiff as a poker—as limp as a glove;
As blind as a bat—as deaf as a post;
As cool as a cucumber—as warm as a toast;
As flat as a flounder—as round as a ball;
As blunt as a hammer—as sharp as an awl;
As red as a ferret—as safe as the stocks;
As bold as a thief—as sly as a fox;
As straight as an arrow—as crook'd as a bow;
As yellow as saffron—as black as a sloe;
As brittle as glass—as tough as gristle;
As neat as my nail—as clean as a whistle;
As good as a feast—as bad as a witch;
As light as is day—as dark as is pitch;
As brisk as a bee—as dull as an ass;
As full as a tick—as solid as brass.

Fascinating Facts about the United States

From *The Story of Our Post Office* by MARSHALL CUSHING

Note: These "facts" may no longer be true, but they were back in the 1890's when the data was prepared for "The Story of Our Post Office."

There are 33 states that have post offices bearing the name of Washington. Thirty states have post offices named Lincoln; 23 Grant; 21 Blaine; 22 Logan; 24 Sherman; 22 Sheridan; 28 Jackson; 17 Hancock; 14 Custer; 25 Cleveland; 6 Hendricks; 7 Tilden; 8 Hayes; 9 Thomas; 6 Dorsey; 13 Chase; 3 Polk; 1 McClellan.

Alice is the name of 10 post offices; Alma, 22; Alpha, 18. There are 22 Arcadias, 26 Ashlands, 20 Avons, 25 Belmonts, and 26 Berlins. The shortest name in the *Guide* is B, in Tippecanoe County, Indiana. There is one Apple. Bowl, Brick, Bee and Box are in the list. In 9 states a post office is named Bliss. There are Blue Eyes, Blue Jackets and Blue Blankets, Blacks and Blackbirds.

Mary has 1 post office: Lucy, 2; Laura, 2; the Larks have 4; Kate, 1, and Kathleen, 4; Jump, 2; Jumbo, 7; John, 4, and John Day, 1; James, 6; Edith, 8; Edna, 4; Cora, 11; Francis, 9; Frank, 7; Grace, 7; Emma, 9; Fannie, 2; Flat, 1. There are 2 High, 3 Sugar, 3 Coffee, and 1 Cream, with 2 Creameries; 1 Wig; 2 Wing; 1 Worry; 1 Pay-up; 4 Cash; 3 Cave; 3 Confidence, 1 Confusion and 1 Confederate, and 1 Cool-Well.

It has been pointed out that the religious enthusiast may select from any of the following: Eden, Paradise, Baptistown, Brick-Church, Canaan, Genesis, Jerusalem, Land of Promise, New Hope, Old Hundred, Pray, Promised Land, Old Church, Sabbath Rest, Zion, Bible Grove, Churches (three), Stone Church, and Saints Rest.

The military genius could be suited at Battle Ground, Broken Sword, Cavalry, Camp Ground, Canon Store, Encampment, Little Warrior, Headquarters, Warrior's Mark, Seven Guns, Stewart's Draft, Tenth Legion, Union Camp, or Warrior's Stand.

The baseball maniac would be interested in Ball Play, Ball Ton, Catchall, Two Runs, Umpire, Best Pitch, Six Runs, or Ball Ground, and the medical profession is recalled when these towns are named: Colon, Doctor Town, All Healing, Cureall, Healing Spring, Medicine Lodge, Mount Healthy and Water Cure. It has been pointed out by another that there are at least two offices in the United States where the above Mosaics should be noted with especial interest. They are Rat, Alabama, and Chestnut Hill, Mass.

The Great Ones Believed in Brevity

An observation by Thomas Jefferson

Our body was little numerous, but very contentious. Day after day was wasted on the most unimportant questions. [A member] was one of those afflicted with the morbid rage of debate, of an ardent mind, prompt imagination, and copious flow of words, he heard with impatience any logic which was not his own. Sitting near me on some occasion of a trifling but wordy debate, [he] asked me how I could sit in silence hearing so much false reasoning which a word should refute? I observed to him that to refute was easy, but to silence impossible; that in measures brought forward by myself, I took the laboring oar, as was incumbent on me; but that in general I was willing to listen. . . .

I served with General Washington in the legislature of Virginia before the revolution, and, during it, with Dr. Franklin in Congress. I never heard either of them speak ten minutes at a time, nor on any but the main point which was to decide the question. They laid their shoulders to the great points, knowing that the little ones would follow of themselves. If the present Congress errs in too much talking, how can it be otherwise in a body to which the people send 150 lawyers, whose trade it is to question everything, yield nothing, & talk by the hour? That 150 lawyers should do business together ought not to be expected.

Happiness Reflects Happiness

by Ida Scott Taylor

Happiness is the sunshine of the heart. Its rays dispel the clouds in life's sky, and drive away tempests of doubt and storms of despair. If the heart is full of sunshine, it brims over in the eyes, and flows from the tongue like liquid silver. Happy words are ever welcome words, and blessed is he whose earthly mission is to make cheerful and bright those around him. There is always a corner in every household for the happy guest: the guest who is contented with everything, who demands little, and whose sunny presence is reflected in every face into which he looks. He has a courteous way of smoothing out little difficulties, and of smiling down impatient words, and of seeing the best side of everything. Blessed are the happy-hearted; would that earth had more of them!

* * *

Surely happiness is reflective, . . . and every countenance bright with smiles, and glowing with innocent enjoyment, is a mirror transmitting to others the rays of a supreme and ever-shining benevolence.

—Washington Irving

An effort made for the happiness of others lifts us above ourselves.

—Mrs. L. M. Child

Some Thoughts Concerning the Hometown Paper

One thing which we pretty much take for granted all of our lives is our hometown newspaper. An unknown author didn't take it for granted—and so he wrote these words in honor of it.

There's a little country paper that I love to sit and read,
A paper poorly printed and behind the times indeed;
With its pages small and narrow, and the ink inclined to
    spread,
And here and there a letter gravely standing on its head.

Or caps, a bit erratic, boldly popping into view
In unexpected places, and knocking things askew;
A real old-fashioned paper from my own home town.
Each week I hail its coming and I never put it down,
Till I've read its every column, all the local news, you know,
About the dear old folks I used to live with long ago.
I note whose barn is painted, whose cattle took the prize,
And how Uriah Potts has raised a squash of wondrous size.

How Farmer Martin's daughter takes the school another
    year;
At this I pause and smile a bit, approving her career,
Remembering how, in bygone days, when life seemed made
    for mirth,
I thought this schoolma'am's mother was the sweetest girl
    on earth.

And now and then perchance I read that one I know is
    gone—
Or find some boyhood chum a second wife has taken on;
And so it goes and none can know what memories, sad and
    sweet,
Come back to me whene'er I read this homely little sheet.

Play Song

From *Music* by Henry van Dyke

O lead me by the hand,
    And let my heart have rest,
And bring me back to childhood land,
To find again the long-lost band
    Of playmates blithe and blest.

    Some quaint, old-fashioned air,
    That all the children knew,
Shall run before us everywhere,
Like a little maid with flying hair,
    To guide the merry crew.

    Along the garden ways
    We chase the light-foot tune,
And in and out the flowery maze,
With eager haste and fond delays,
    In pleasant paths of June.

    For us the fields are new,
    For us the woods are rife
With fairy secrets, deep and true,
And heaven is but a tent of blue
    Above the game of life.

    The world is far away:
    The fever and the fret,
And all that makes the heart grow gray,
Is out of sight and far away,
Dear Music, while I hear thee play
That olden, golden roundelay,
    "Remember and forget!"

The Myth of the Communist Superman

by Clarence B. Randall

From *The Folklore of Management*
Copyright, 1959, 1960, 1961, by Clarence B. Randall
with permission of Atlantic-Little, Brown and Company

Our corporations now have about 12.5 million direct share-holders. And if we consider the stock held by pension trusts, insurance companies, and the like, it is probable that over fifty million Americans participate directly in the earnings of our industry. Most large companies now have more stockholders than employees, and by the same token, each year more and more employees become stockholders.

That, in my view, is the most astounding economic revolution in all history. What nonsense, what effrontery to hurl the vulgar epithet "monopolists" at us! What empty boasting to claim that Communists discovered the principle of the people's ownership of the means of production!

Or compare the two systems in accumulation of the capital required to add to the means of production, which further raises the standard of living. What is so novel about the method employed by the Communists? Under their social order, the state merely appropriates to itself the surplus which it re-quires—taking it away from those who have made the effort, without their consent. In the United States, each employed person makes his own decision as to whether he will consume or save. If he chooses thrift, he then makes another individual decision as to what form of investment he favors. The infinite multiplicity of these decisions makes up the force which deter-mines the direction our economy will take. It is ours—not theirs—which is the true "People's Democracy."

The same difference is found when we compare the Com-munist system of education with that in a free America. Every-thing that we do in our schools and colleges is designed to benefit the individual; everything that they do is designed to benefit the state. We try to make it possible for all boys and girls to choose the intellectual discipline which will best suit their talents, as they themselves see those talents, to the end that their lives may be enriched as they advance toward the objectives which they themselves formulate. Not so with Com-munism. The state determines who shall be a scientist, a lawyer,

an artist, or a nurse. If a wrong decision is made, the individual is irrevocably committed to a lifetime of frustration. No escape mechanism is available. This in itself must be a great loss in effectiveness, even for a collective regime. I once knew an apothecary who ultimately became president of a great corporation. In Russia he would have rolled pills and done nothing else till the day of his death. How clear it is that ours is the dynamic way, and theirs the unenlightened!

There is one thing on the positive side to be said about Communism. They are not afflicted with our weakness: they are not afraid to study our system. Soviet libraries undoubtedly contain many authentic works on capitalism, and there can be no doubt that Soviet economists keep abreast of current American writing in the field of trade and production. When they engage in dialectics with visiting American businessmen, it is they, not we, who are the better informed.

There is hope for the future in that, even against their will, they are being driven by implacable economic circumstance to move away from their basic philosophy toward ours. Karl Marx must be spinning rather violently in his grave these days. "To each man according to his need, and from each man according to his ability" is steadily giving way to reward proportionate to effort. The direct application of the principle of incentives is spreading rapidly throughout the Communist industrial system. In the large plants, at least, the whole unit receives a bonus for output in excess of quota, and within the organization the particular departments have their own group quotas and bonuses. There is also an astonishing spread between the salaries and perquisites that are assigned to the various echelons of authority.

Even with respect to home ownership, there are signs of a crack in their brittle concept of collectivism. It now appears that one of the inducements offered in recruiting workers for new plants in the far reaches of Siberia, where until recently no man has ever gone voluntarily, is the privilege of building or buying a home that may be retained as private property.

Conceivably, too, the production commissars are being compelled to move crudely toward the basic elements of a price system and cost accounting. In their nationwide production line, as a commodity moves from one plant to another for further processing—such as steel to a tractor factory—there obviously has to be some basis for crediting the first plant with output and charging the next with intake. Otherwise the bonus scheme would break down. You have to have a cost to start with if you are to measure the value of the added effort.

Similarly, in the field of foreign trade there has to be at least the crude outline of a price structure, particularly for buyers who deal with both West and East and want to make comparisons. The leaders of proud and highly nationalistic new nations are prone to the suspicion that other countries get a better deal. Communist traders know that to make a better proposition to India than to Burma is not a good way to win friends and influence people.

None of this is meant to suggest for a single moment that Communism is not still a great threat to world peace and to world economic stability. Quite the contrary. In the field of economic penetration the Soviets are tough, resourceful competitors. To hold our place in the world will require strong effort. But there is no cause for panic. They are no supermen. We can beat them, and on our own terms, if we will only fear them less and trust ourselves more.

One lesson we must learn from them, however. We must come to see as clearly as they do what it is that we believe, and must bring to the fulfillment of this revolutionary industrial faith of ours the same dedication of spirit and the same tirelessness of effort that they display in propagating theirs.

Preparing for the Later Years

Written about 52 B. C. by MARCUS TULLIUS CICERO

We must prepare ourselves, my friends, against old age; and as it is advancing endeavor by our diligence to mitigate and correct the natural infirmities that attend it. We must use proper preservatives, as we do against diseases. Great care must, in the first place, be taken of our health; all bodily exercise must be moderate, and especially our diet; which ought to be of such a kind, and in such proportion, as may refresh and strengthen nature, without oppressing it. Nor must our care be confined to our bodies only: for the mind requires much more, which, without it will not only decay, but our understanding will as certainly die away in old age, as a lamp not duly supplied with oil. The body, we know, when over-labored, becomes heavy, and, as it were, jaded; but 'tis exercise alone that supports the spirits, and keeps the mind in vigor. Hence it is, that you see old men disadvantageously represented by Caecilius, and other comic poets on the stage, when the characters of weak and credulous, or dissolute old fellows, are exposed to contempt and ridicule.

But these are the vices only of such as, when grey with years, abandon themselves to idleness and extravagance, and not of old age itself. For as wantonness and loose desires are more peculiar to youth than to the aged; and yet not to all youth, but to such only as are by nature viciously inclined, or have been loosely educated; so that silly dotishness, that is imputed to old age, will be found only in persons of weak and abject spirits. Appius had four stout sons, and five daughters; yet though he was very old, and blind besides, he was able not only to govern that great family, but also to manage his large dependencies of clients: he kept his mind ever intent upon his affairs, without flagging or bending under his age, and maintaining not only an authority, but a command over his people: his servants stood in awe of him; his children revered him, and they all loved him; and that whole family constantly kept up to the sober and strict discipline derived to them by succession from their ancestors. Thus old age is ever honorable, where it takes care to support its proper rights, and gives them not weakly away, but asserts them to the last.

The Meaning of the American Flag

Many eloquent speeches have been made that recite what the flag should stand for to a citizen of America. Among them one is here selected from an address by the Reverend Henry Ward Beecher to members of the Fourteenth Regiment of New York State Troops in 1861.

As at the early dawn the stars shine forth even while it grows light, and then, as the sun advances, that light breaks into banks and streaming lines of color, the glowing red and intense white striving together and ribbing the horizon with bars effulgent; so, on the American flag, stars and beams of many-colored light shine out together. . . .

It is the banner of dawn. It means *Liberty*; and the galley slave, the poor oppressed conscript, the down-trodden creature of foreign despotism, sees in the American flag that very promise and production of God: "The people which sat in darkness, saw a great light; and to them which sat in the region and shadow of death, light is sprung up."

In 1777, within a few days of one year after the Declaration of Independence, the congress of the colonies in the confederated states assembled and ordained this glorious national flag which we now hold and defend, and advanced it full high before God and all men as the flag of liberty. It was no holiday flag gorgeously emblazoned for gayety or vanity. It was a solemn national symbol. . . .

Our flag carries American ideas, American history, and American feelings. Beginning with the colonies, and coming down to our time, in its sacred heraldry, in its glorious insignia, it has gathered and stored chiefly this supreme idea: *Divine right of liberty in man.* Every color means liberty; every thread means liberty; every form of star and beam or stripe of light means liberty; not lawlessness, not license; but organized, institutional liberty—liberty through law, and laws for liberty!

It is not a painted rag. It is a whole national history. It is the Constitution. It is the Government. It is the free people that stand in the government on the Constitution.

Concord Hymn

July 4, 1837

by RALPH WALDO EMERSON

By the rude bridge that arched the flood,
　Their flag to April's breeze unfurled,
Here once the embattled farmers stood
　And fired the shot heard round the world.

The foe long since in silence slept;
　Alike the conqueror silent sleeps;
And Time the ruined bridge has swept
　Down the dark stream which seaward creeps.

On this green bank, by this soft stream,
　We set today a votive stone;
That memory may their deed redeem,
　When, like our sires, our sons are gone.

Spirit, that made those heroes dare
　To die, and leave their children free,
Bid Time and Nature gently spare
　The shaft we raise to them and thee.

Give Some Meaning to Education

From a lecture given by JOHN DEWEY in 1900

Our social life has undergone a thorough and radical change. If our education is to have any meaning for life, it must pass through an equally complete transformation. This transformation is not something to appear suddenly, to be executed in a day by conscious purpose. It is already in progress. Those modifications of our school system which often appear (even to those most actively concerned with them, to say nothing of their spectators) to be mere changes of detail, mere improvement within the school mechanism, are in reality signs and evidences of evolution.

The introduction of active occupations, of nature study, of elementary science, of art, of history; the relegation of the merely symbolic and formal to a secondary position; the change in the moral school atmosphere, in the relation of pupils and teachers—of discipline; the introduction of more active, expressive, and self-directing factors—all these are not mere accidents, they are necessities of the larger social evolution. It remains but to organize all these factors, to appreciate them in their fullness of meaning, and to put the ideas and ideals involved into complete, uncompromising possession of our school system. To do this means to make each one of our schools an embryonic community life, active with types of occupations that reflect the life of the larger society, and permeated throughout with the spirit of art, history, and science. When the school introduces and trains each child of society into membership within such a little community, saturating him with the spirit of service, and providing him with the instruments of effective self-direction, we shall have the deepest and best guarantee of a larger society which is worthy, lovely, and harmonious.

A Loving Thought

by EMILY DICKINSON

From *Bolts of Melody, New Poems of Emily Dickinson*
Copyright, 1945 by the Trustees of Amherst College
Published by Harper & Row, Publishers

We learned the whole of love,
The alphabet, the words,
A chapter, then the mighty book—
Then revelation closed.

But in each other's eyes
An ignorance beheld
Diviner than the childhood's,
And each to each a child

Attempted to expound
What neither understood.
Alas, that wisdom is so large
And truth so manifold!

All Things Have Their Season

From *The Complete Works of Montaigne*, translated by DONALD M. FRAME
Copyright 1948, 1957, 1958
by the Board of Trustees of the Leland Stanford Junior University
Published by Stanford University Press

I have lived, and run out the course that fortune gave.

—VIRGIL

In short, this is all the comfort that I find in my old age, that it deadens in me many desires and cares by which life is troubled —care for how the world goes, care for riches, for greatness, for knowledge, for health, for myself. That man* is learning to speak when he needs to learn to be silent forever.

We may continue our studies at all times, but not our schooling: what a foolish thing is an old man learning his A B C!

Different men, different tastes; nor are all things
Fit for all ages.

—MAXIMIANUS

If we must study, let us study something suitable to our condition, so that we may answer like the man who, when he was asked what was the purpose of these studies in his decrepitude, replied: "To depart a better man and more content."

Such a study was that of the *younger* Cato when, feeling his end approaching, he came upon Plato's discussion of the eternity of the soul. Not, obviously, that he had not been long furnished with every sort of equipment for such a departure. Of assurance, firm will, and learning, he had more than Plato has in his writings; his knowledge and his courage were in this regard above philosophy. It was not to ease his death that he took up this occupation; but like a man who would not even interrupt his sleep out of concern over such a resolve, he also continued, without choice and without change, his studies together with the other customary actions of his life.

The night when he had just been rejected for the praetorship, he spent in play; the one in which he was to die, he spent reading. Loss of life and loss of office were equally indifferent to him.

*Cato the Censor, learning Greek in his old age.

· 44 ·

Bits of Philosophy from Ancient Scholars

The face, when we are born, is no less tender than any other part of the body: it is use alone hardens it, and makes it more able to endure the cold. And therefore the Scythian philosopher gave a very significant answer to the Athenian, who wondered how he could go naked in frost and snow.

"How," said the Scythian, "can you endure your face exposed to the sharp winter?"

"My face is used to it," said the Athenian.

"Think me all face," replied the Scythian.

Our bodies will endure anything, that from the beginning they are accustomed to.

From *Some Thoughts Concerning Education* by John Locke

* * * * *

We have no just quarrel with Nature, for leaving us naked; or to envy the Horns, Hoofs, Skins, and Furs of other creatures, being provided with Reason, that can supply them all.

From *Religio Medici* by Sir Thomas Browne

* * * * *

How little can be known—
This is the wise man's sigh; how far we err—
This is the good man's not infrequent pang!
And they perhaps err least, the lowly class
Whom a benign necessity compels
To follow Reason's least ambitious course;
Such do I mean who, unperplexed by doubt
And unincited by a wish to look
Into high objects farther than they may,
Pace to and fro, from morn till even-tide,
The narrow avenue of daily toil
For daily bread.

From *The Excursion* by William Wordsworth

Nor stony tower, nor walls of beaten brass,
Nor airless dungeon, nor strong links of iron,
Can be retentive to the strength of spirit;
But life, being weary of these worldly bars,
Never lacks power to dismiss itself. . . .
So every bondman in his own hand bears
The power to cancel his captivity.

From Julius Caesar (I, iii) by Shakespeare

* * * * *

I will not give a penny for a life,
Nor half a halfpenny to shun grim death,
Since for to live is but to seek to die,
And dying but beginning of new life.
Let come the hour when he that rules it will!
To live, or die, I hold indifferent.

Author not traced

* * * * *

Never Bite the Hand that Helps You
by JOHN WEBSTER

Stay, my lord: I'll tell you a tale. The crocodile
which lives in the river Nilus, hath a worm breeds
i' the teeth of 't, which puts it to extreme anguish:
a little bird, no bigger than a wren, is barber-surgeon
to this crocodile; flies into the jaws of 't, picks out
the worm, and brings present remedy. The fish, glad
of ease, but ingrateful to her that did it, that the
bird may not talk largely of her abroad for non-
payment, closeth her chops, intending to swallow
her, and so put her to perpetual silence. But nature
loathing such ingratitude, hath armed this bird with
a quill or prick in the head, the top o' which wounds
the crocodile i' the mouth, forceth her to open her
bloody prison, and away flies the pretty tooth-picker
from her cruel patient.

From The White Devil—1612

The Opinion of Others Can Be Very Misleading

by JOHN LOCKE

There is another, I confess, which, though by itself it be no true ground of probability, yet is often made use of for one, by which men most commonly regulate their assent, and upon which they pin their faith more than anything else, and that is the opinion of others: though there cannot be a more dangerous thing to rely on, nor more likely to mislead one; since there is much more falsehood and error among men, than truth and knowledge. And if the opinions and persuasions of others, whom we know and think well of, be a ground of assent, men have reason to be Heathens in Japan, Mahometans in Turkey, Papists in Spain, Protestants in England, and Lutherans in Sweden. But of this wrong ground of assent I shall have occasion to speak more at large in another place. . . .

Any testimony, the farther off it is from the original truth, the less force and proof it has. The being and existence of the thing itself is what I call the original truth. A credible man vouching his knowledge of it is a good proof: but if another equally credible do witness it from his report, the testimony is weaker; and a third that attests the hear-say of an hear-say, is yet less considerable. So that in traditional truths, each remove weakens the force of the proof; and the more hands the tradition has successively passed through, the less strength and evidence does it receive from them.

This I thought necessary to be taken notice of, because I find amongst some men the quite contrary commonly practised, who look on opinions to gain force by growing older; and what a thousand years since would not, to a rational man, contemporary with the first voucher, have appeared at all probable, is now urged as certain beyond all question, only because several have since, from him, said it one after another. Upon this ground, propositions, evidently false or doubtful enough in their first beginning, come by an inverted rule of probability to pass for authentic truths; and those which found or deserved little credit from the mouths of their first authors, are thought to grow venerable by age, and are urged as undeniable.

From *An Essay Concerning Human Understanding*

Post Office Problems Before the Zip Code

by Marshall Cushing

In a big city like Chicago, of course, thousands and thousands of letters are received where it is almost impossible to make out the addresses. One of the Chicago clerks has tabulated the different spellings of Chicago; and he finds without much trouble that they numbered one hundred and ninety-seven. Only a short time ago a Finnish letter writer addressed his brother at Zizazo; and other spellings in the list were: Jagjago, Hipaho, Jajijo, Schechacho, Hizago, and Chachicho. Then wrong addresses are given, and great difficulty is found in finding the person for whom the letter or paper was intended.

Several months ago a paper was addressed to Mrs. M. Kracky, 612 Dixon Street, but the carrier could not find her. All the people interested were Polanders, including the carrier, and they had a time of it. Here is the carrier's story in his own report:

> Mrs. M. Kracky does not live at 612 Dixon Street. Six hundred and twelve Dickson is a two-story house, occupied by four families, to wit: On the first floor in front lives Mr. Pafelski, an uncle of Mrs. Kracky; with him also lives his mother, or grandmother to Mrs. Kracky; above them lives Mr. Riszewski. In the rear on the top floor lives Mrs. Kilichowski, and below her lives Mrs. Pinkowski, a mother of Mrs. Kracky, whom the latter calls on about twice a month, more or less.
>
> Now, when this January number came to me I am positive that I asked three times in front of both families, and I am also positive that I opened Mrs. Pinkowski's door at least twice and asked there, as I had to pass her door four times in order to see Mrs. Kilichowski, who was asleep twice. The third time she was out, the fourth time I got her at home, and each time I called out the name loud enough for Mrs. Pinkowski to hear.
>
> The November number I must have delivered in October, but I can't remember it. The December number was delivered by the substitute, as I was on my annual vacation from Nov. 1 to Nov. 16.
>
> To-day as I called there Mrs. Kracky happened to be there washing for her mother, and I delivered her magazine. Mrs. M. Kracky, whose proper name is Mrs. M. Krajecki, lives at 596 Holt Street.

What Is a Statesman?

by Charles A. Beard

From *The American Mercury*, April, 1924

A man may be well equipped with powerful engines of logic and controversy and well stocked with knowledge, and yet, if he runs against the current of the long time, he passes away as grass that withers. How many read Bossuet now? And yet Bossuet was infinitely superior in intellect to Rousseau. Madison was one of the brainiest men in our Homeric Age; how many regard him as a statesman? In supercilious Boston he is more often remembered as the author of Mr. Madison's War which prevented business from going on as usual.

If not brains, then is it morals? Well, Mr. Bryan's character is above reproach. Would anyone put him higher in the scale of fame than Benjamin Franklin, whose morals, to speak softly, were marred by a certain carelessness? Is it ideals clung to unflinchingly until death? For every martyr who achieves fame there are a thousand cranks stoned by the mob and consigned to oblivion.

After this negative review, let me hazard a guess. The statesman is one who divines the long future, foresees the place of his class and nation in it, labors intelligently to prepare his countrymen for their fate, combines courage with discretion, takes risks, has good luck, exercises caution where it is necessary, and goes off the stage with a reasonable degree of respectability. He must have brains — some, at least. He must have morals — some, at least. He must have ideals — but only those which are justified in the economy of Providence. He must be able to reconcile himself without complaining to the inexorable movement which the skeptical call the grand *pis aller [last resource]* and the devout the divine plan. He must not only see; he must appear to be achieving in the current of things. Above all, he must be justified by events, that is, by good fortune. Perhaps beyond reason and understanding both Carlyle and Marx may be reconciled, a little bit. Meanwhile the mystery must not be entirely cleared up. Otherwise the game of politics would lose its savor.

William Tell, Patriot and Father

by EMILY DICKINSON

From *Bolts of Melody, New Poems of Emily Dickinson*
Copyright, 1945 by the Trustees of Amherst College
Published by Harper & Row, Publishers

Tell as a marksman were forgotten,
Tell this day endures
Ruddy as that coeval apple
The tradition bears.

Fresh as mankind that humble story,
Though a statelier tale
Grown in the repetition hoary
Scarcely could prevail.

Tell had a son—the ones that knew it
Need not linger here;
Those who do not, to human nature
Will subscribe a tear.

Tell would not bare his head in presence
Of the ducal hat,
Threatened for that with death by Gessler,
Tyranny bethought

Make of his only boy a target—
That surpasses death.
Stolid to love's supreme entreaty,
Not forsook of faith,

Mercy of the Almighty begging,
Tell his arrow sent.
God it is said replies in person
When the cry is meant.

∽

Advice to His Godson in a Letter from Lord Chesterfield

Two things are absolutely necessary for every young man who has a laudable ambition to make a figure in the world. They are learning and politeness, and they should always go together; for learning without politeness makes a disagreeable pedant, and politeness without learning makes a superficial, frivolous puppy. I am sorry to say that in general the youth of the present age have neither. Their manners are illiberal, and their ignorance is notorious. They are sportsmen, they are jockeys, they know nor love nothing but dogs and horses, racing and hunting. They seem even afraid of being taken for gentlemen, and therefore dress themselves like blackguards. This gives you a fine opportunity of distinguishing yourself among your growing contemporaries, and should you even fall short of perfection, you will still shine; for you know the French saying, *that in the country of the blind the one-eyed are kings.*

Interpretations Differ

Moral words are in most men's mouths little more than bare sounds; or when they have any, it is for the most part but a very loose and undetermined, and consequently obscure and confused significa-tion. . . . Where shall one find any, either contro-versial debate, or familiar discourse, concerning honour, faith, grace, religion, church, etc., wherein it is not easy to observe the different notions men have of them? . . . And hence we see, that in the interpretation of laws, whether divine or human, there is no end; comments beget comments; and explications make new matter for explications. . . . Many a man who was pretty well satisfied of the meaning of a text of scripture, or clause in the code at first reading, has by consulting commentators quite lost the sense of it, and by these elucidations given rise or increase to his doubts, and drawn obscurity upon the place.

From *An Essay Concerning Human Understanding* by John Locke

*   *   *   *   *

Old things need not be therefore true,
O brother men, nor yet the new;
Ah! still awhile the old thought retain,
And yet consider it again.

The souls of now two thousand years
Have laid up here their toils and fears,
And all the earnings of their pain,—
Ah, yet consider it again.

—A. H. Clough

*   *   *   *   *

I have learned and from an author of unquestion-able authority that even the mending of a state is not worth the disordering and troubling of it.

From *Private Memoirs 1628* by Sir Kenelm Digby

A FABLE

by Ella Wheeler Wilcox

Some cawing Crows, a hooting Owl,
A Hawk, a Canary, an old Marsh-Fowl,
   One day all met together,
To hold a caucus and settle the fate
Of a certain bird (without a mate),
   A bird of another feather.

"My friends," said the Owl, with a look most wise,
"The Eagle is soaring too near the skies,
   In a way that is quite improper;
Yet the world is praising her, so I'm told,
And I think her actions have grown so bold
   That some of us ought to stop her."

"I have heard it said," quoth Hawk, with a sigh,
"That young lambs died at the glance of her eye,
   And I wholly scorn and despise her.
This, and more, I am told they say—
And I think that the only proper way
   Is never to recognize her."

"I am quite convinced," said Crow, with a caw.
"That the Eagle minds no moral law
  She's a most unruly creature."
"She's an ugly thing," piped Canary Bird;
"Some call her handsome — it's so absurd —
  She hasn't a decent feature."

Then the old Marsh Hen went hopping about,
She said she was sure — *she* hadn't a doubt —
  Of the truth of each bird's story;
And she thought it a duty to stop her flight,
To pull her down from her lofty height,
  And take the gilt from her glory.

But, lo! from a peak on the mountain grand
That looks out over the smiling land
  And over the mighty ocean,
The Eagle is spreading her splendid wings —
She rises, rises, and upward swings,
  With a slow, majestic motion.

Up in the blue of God's own skies,
With a cry of rapture, away she flies,
  Close to the Great Eternal:
She sweeps the world with her piercing sight —
Her soul is filled with the Infinite
  And the joy of things supernal.

Thus rise forever the chosen of God,
The genius-crowned or the power-shod,
  Over the dust-world sailing;
And back, like splinters blown by the winds,
Must fall the missiles of silly minds,
  Useless and unavailing.

"It was God who inspired the American Constitution"

as expressed by an English historian in 1815

Unawed by the arbitrary mandate of a master, uncramped by the imperious will and command of a tyrant, he can call himself and his possessions *his own*. The operations of his mind are free; he can reason upon the subjects of religion and civil government and publish his sentiments without control; and choose his own religion and his own legislator; without being compelled to support a sect or profession he cannot with a good conscience embrace, or to obey a law that he has not by his representatives given his consent to.

Other nations may be mentioned, which possess a fine climate, a rich soil, valuable produce of every kind; but divested of the civil and religious rights of man.

Where is the country (America excepted) that possesses a free representative government? Where is the country, that is not more or less encumbered with a civil establishment in religion? It is the peculiar excellence of the American Constitution, that it not only possesses a general representative government, but that every particular state has its own distinct legislature within itself. This preserves a proper equilibrium, answers every purpose of security, protection and defence, and seems to promise stability and long duration. America has set an instructive example to the world, that religion may exist, may prosper and flourish, without the aid of a civil establishment.

How many churches have been erected, and are supported in this city, and elsewhere, by the voluntary donations and contributions of individuals! How pleasing, how exceedingly gratifying is it to a generous and philanthropic mind to behold them all on an equal footing—to think that the richest and most numerous sects enjoy no legal privileges or prerogatives above the smallest and the least opulent, that none are guarded by test or corporation acts, that none exist only by connivance or permission, that all are equally under the protection of the laws of the state, and that *intoleration* is unknown in this *happy country*.

It was God who preserved and protected the first settlers in this country, when they were comparatively few, and struggling almost under unsurmountable difficulties. Under his guardian and fostering hand they grew up and flourished, and converted woods and deserts into fruitful lands. It was God who carried our countrymen honourably and successfully through the hard and difficult trials and conflicts of the revolutionary war. He *saved* them with a mighty *salvation*. He was the *shield of their help* and *the sword of their excellency*. It was God who inspired and directed their wise men to form good and estimable Constitutions, and establish a system of civil and religious liberty which may justly challenge the admiration of the world. It was the same almighty and merciful Being who *saved* us in the late war, who covered the heads of our dear countrymen in the day of battle, infused courage, skill and activity into the minds of our warriors by sea and land, and granted us so many splendid victories over our enemies. This *salvation* appears still the more *illustrious* when we take into consideration, that by a strange and unexpected revolution in the affairs of Europe, the most war-like and best disciplined troops of a powerful nation, highly exasperated, were sent against us, and yet were foiled and defeated in repeated actions, by men lately raised and little accustomed to martial operations.

These are only a few of the many mercies and favours conferred upon our country by a kind Providence, for which may we ever prove grateful.

★ ★ ★ ★ ★

Let no flatterer persuade your lordship, that the Americans are to be either wheedled or corrupted, They love *peace;* but they are a wise people, and they will well know that they must provide for war. The last year has taught them that they must depend solely on their arms. They will remember the flames of Frenchtown, Stonington and Washington. They will remember their sufferings from the hand of our Indian allies. They will remember our considering their naturalized citizens as traitors.

— Stated in 1815, after the War of 1812,
by William Cobbett, an English historian

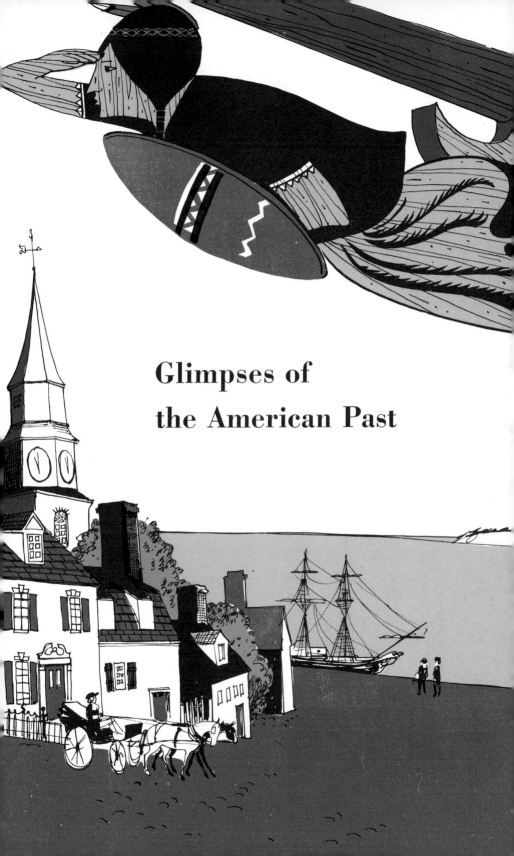

Glimpses of
the American Past

The Coast of Maine

as Viewed by a French Journalist in 1556

From *The History of Maine* by John S. C. Abbott, a native of the state

In the year 1556, a French gentleman by the name of André Thevet, a scholar and a writer of much repute, desiring to see the New World, took passage in a vessel which sailed along the entire east coast of both South and North America. Thevet visited the coast of Maine, and gives the following description of the Penobscot River: —

Here we entered a river which is one of the finest in the whole world. We call it Norumbega. It is marked on some charts as the Grand River. The natives call it Agoncy. Several beautiful rivers flow into it. Upon its banks the French formerly erected a small fort, about ten leagues from its mouth. It was called the Fort of Norumbega, and was surrounded by fresh water.

Before you enter this river, there appears an island surrounded by eight small islets. These are near the country of the Green Mountains. About three leagues into the river, there is an island four leagues in circumference, which the natives call Aiayascon. It would be easy to plant on this island, and to build a fortress, which would hold in check the whole surrounding country. Upon landing, we saw a great multitude of people coming down upon us in such numbers that you might have supposed them to be a flight of starlings. The men came first, then the women, then the boys, then the girls. They were all clothed in the skins of wild animals.

Considering their aspect, and mode of advancing, we mistrusted them, and retired on board our vessel. They, perceiving our fear, made signs of friendship. The better to assure us, they sent to our vessel several of their principal men, with presents of provisions. We returned a few trinkets of little value, with which they were highly pleased. The next morning, I, with some others, was commissioned to meet them, to see if we could obtain more provisions, of which we stood in great need. As we entered the house of the chief, who was called Peramick, we saw several slaughtered animals hanging on the beams.

The chief gave us a hearty welcome. To show his affection he ordered a fire to be built, on which meat and fish were placed to be roasted. Upon this some warriors came in, bringing to

The coast of Maine off Campobello Island at the entrance of the Passamaquoddy Bay.

the chief the dissevered heads of six men whom they had taken in battle. The sight terrified us. Fearing that we might suffer in the same way, we, towards evening, secretly retired to our ship, without bidding our host good-by.

This greatly displeased him. In the morning he came to the ship with three of his children. His countenance was very sad, for he thought he had offended us. He said to me, in his own language,—

"Go back on land with me, my friend and brother. Come and eat and drink such as we have. We assure you upon oath, by heaven, earth, moon, and stars, that you shall not fare worse than we do ourselves."

Seeing the good affection of this old man, twenty of us went again on land, all well armed. We went to his house, where we were feasted, and presented with whatever he possessed. Meanwhile large numbers of his people arrived. They all greeted us in the most affectionate manner, declaring that they were our friends. Late in the evening, when we wished to retire, they all entreated us to remain through the night. But we could not be persuaded to sleep with them. And so we retired to our vessel. Having remained in this place five days, we weighed anchor, and, parting from them with a marvellous contentment on both sides, went out upon the open sea.

Observations on American Life and Growth in the Colonial Period

Written in Pennsylvania in 1751 by Benjamin Franklin

People increase in proportion to the number of marriages, and that is greater, in proportion to the ease and convenience of supporting a family. When families can be easily supported, more persons marry, and earlier in life.

In cities, where all trades, occupations, and offices, are full, many delay marrying, till they can see how to bear the charges of a family; which charges are greater in cities, as luxury is more common. Many live single during life, and continue servants to families, journeymen to trade, etc. Hence cities do not, by natural generation, supply themselves with inhabitants. The deaths are more than the births.

In heavily populated countries, the case must be nearly the same, all lands being occupied and improved to the maximum. Those who cannot get land must labor for others that have it. When laborers are plenty, their wages will be low. By low wages a family is supported with difficulty; this difficulty deters many from marriage, who therefore long continue servants and single. Only as the cities take supplies of people from the country, and thereby make a little more room in the country, marriage is a little more encouraged there, and the births exceed the deaths.

A great part of Europe is fully settled with husbandmen, manufacturers, etc., and therefore cannot now much increase in people. America is chiefly occupied by Indians, who subsist mostly by hunting. But as the hunter, of all men, requires the greatest quantity of land from whence to draw his subsistence, (the farmer subsisting on much less, the gardener on still less, and the manufacturer requiring least of all) the Europeans found America as fully settled, as it well could be, by hunters. Yet these, having large tracts, were easily prevailed on to part with portions of territory to the newcomers, who did not much interfere with the natives in hunting, and furnished them with many things they wanted.

Land being thus plentiful in America, and so cheap, a laboring man that understands farming can, in a short time, save money enough to purchase a piece of new land, sufficient for a plantation, whereon he may support a family. Such are not afraid to marry, for if they even look far enough forward to

consider how their children, when grown up, are to be provided for, they see that more land is to be had at rates equally easy, all circumstances considered.

Hence marriages in America are more general, and more generally early, than in Europe. And if it is reckoned there, that there is but one marriage *per annum* among 100 persons, perhaps we may here reckon two, and if in Europe, they have but four births to a marriage, (many of their marriages being late) we may here reckon eight, of which, if one half grow up, and our marriages are made, on an average, at twenty years of age, our people must at least be doubled every twenty years.

But notwithstanding this increase, so vast is the territory of North America, that it will require many ages to settle it fully, and till it is fully settled, labor will never be cheap here, where no man continues long a laborer for others, but gets a plantation of his own. No man continues long a journeyman to a trade, but goes among those new settlers, and sets up for himself. Hence labor is no cheaper now, in Pennsylvania, than it was thirty years ago, though so many thousand laboring people have been imported from Germany and Ireland.

As the increase of people depends on the encouragement of marriages, the following things must diminish a nation.

1. The being conquered; for the conquerors will engross as many offices, and exact as much tribute or profit on the labor of the conquered, as will maintain them in their new establishment; and this diminishing the substance of the natives discourages their marriages, and so gradually diminishes them, while the foreigners increase.

2. Loss of territory.

3. Loss of trade: manufactures, exported, draw subsistence from foreign countries for numbers, who are thereby enabled

to marry and raise families. If the nation be deprived of any branch of trade, and no new employment is found for the people occupied in that branch, it will soon be deprived of so many people.

4. Loss of food. Suppose a nation has a fishery, which not only employs great numbers, but makes the food and subsistence of the people cheaper. If another nation becomes master of the seas, and prevents the fishery, the people will diminish in proportion as the loss of employ and dearness of provision makes it more difficult to subsist a family.

5. Bad government and insecure property. People not only leave such a country, and, settling abroad, incorporate with other nations, lose their native language, and become foreigners; but the industry of those that remain being discouraged, the quantity of subsistence in the country is lessened, and the support of a family becomes more difficult. So heavy taxes tend to diminish a people.

6. The introduction of slaves. The negroes brought into the English sugar islands have greatly diminished the whites there; the poor are by this means deprived of employment, while a few families acquire vast estates, which they spend on foreign luxuries; and educating their children in the habit of those luxuries, the same income is needed for the support of one, that might have maintained one hundred. The whites, who have slaves, not laboring, are enfeebled, and therefore not so generally prolific. The slaves being worked too hard, and ill fed, their constitutions are broken, and the deaths among them are more than the births, so that a continual supply is needed from Africa. The northern colonies, having few slaves, increase in whites. Slaves also pejorate the families that use them. The white children become proud, disgusted with labor, and, being educated in idleness, are rendered unfit to get a living by industry.

Hence the prince, that acquires new territory, if he finds it vacant, or removes the natives to give his own people room;— the legislator, that makes effectual laws for promoting of trade, increasing employment, improving land by more or better tillage, providing more food by fisheries, securing property, etc.— and the man that invents new trades, arts or manufactures, or new improvements in husbandry, may be properly called *fathers of their nation*, as they are the cause of the generation of multitudes, by the encouragement they afford to marriage.

The New York City
of Two Centuries Ago

as described by St. John de Crèvecoeur

The City of New York is beautiful although irregular. This irregularity arises from the nature of the ground, and the steepness of the Peninsula upon which the first houses were built as much as from the necessity of making artificial soil to enlarge the extent of the City, and procure for trade the necessary warehouses and wharves. The inhabitants owe this taste for building over the water to the early Dutch, but to their own intelligence their remarkable skill in execution.

I do not think there are any cities on this Continent where the art of constructing wharves has been pushed to a further extent. I have seen them made in forty feet of water. This is done with the trunks of pines attached together, which they gradually sink, fill in with stones, and cover the surface with earth. Beaver street, to-day so far from the seashore, was so called because formerly it was a little bay, where these animals made a dike. I have talked with old inhabitants, who have seen the tide rise to the neighborhood of the City Hall. You know that is more than four hundred fathoms from the sea. I know an old woman, who told me she had been whipped while a child for stealing apples in an orchard, which stood on the site now occupied by this same City Hall.

Several of the streets have side walks on the two sides, paved with flat stones and ornamented with plane trees, the shade of which in the Summer time is equally beneficial to the foot passers and houses. Here is found Dutch neatness, combined with English taste and architecture; the houses are finished, planned and painted with the greatest care; the merchants are intelligent, able and rich, and the artisans extremely skillful, especially the carpenters, cabinet makers and joiners. Stone being scarce nearly the whole town is built of brick.

Let those who, like myself, have experienced the extent to which the inhabitants of this city push hospitality render them the justice they deserve. New York being the fixed rendezvous of the English Packet ships, this City is necessarily the first where Europeans land; the reception they receive there is quite sufficient to give them a high idea of American generosity as well as of the simple and cordial affability they will meet with in the other towns of the Continent.

Food is cheap and abundant

I know no place where food of every kind is cheaper and more abundant; meat, pork, ham, mutton, butter, cheese, flour, fish, and oysters, all combine to render living wholesome and reasonable; thus everybody lives in comfort, every one is nurtured on excellent food, the poorest laborer not even excepted. I could name you twenty-four different kinds of shell fish and fifty-seven of fish proper; each season furnishes a variety, which appears only for a short period. Each fishing smack is always followed by a very small boat, made of cedar wood, and full of holes. It is in these travelling reservoirs that all the fish come to the New York market. The quantity of oysters which are brought here from every quarter is surprising; all the great bays of Long Island, as well as the harbor, are full of them; they are ordinarily worth 36 sous the hundred.

The streets are often cleaned, and are lighted in dark nights. The houses number three thousand four hundred; there are twenty-eight thousand inhabitants, and twenty churches belonging to different sects.

It is a pleasure to see the College with its beautiful architecture. It is supplied with a good Library and a large number of mathematical instruments of great value. It is only to be regretted that this new Academy was not built far away from the capital, in some rural retreat, where the scholars could be kept from the turmoil of trade, and the dissipations and pleasures always numerous in large cities.

There has been lately built at a proper distance from the City, on elevated ground not far from the Hudson River, a magnificent Hospital for Sailors, the architecture, situation and arrangement of which are an honor to the good citizens, who founded, and the Legislative body which founded it. It is a public Institution, incorporated by an Act of the Assembly, and managed by persons who are elected. After the amounts supposed to be requisite were advanced by the subscribers, the Assembly of the Province granted it a considerable supplement.

A Delightful Description of Colonial Entertaining

From a letter by Laurence Butler to an English friend

Westmoreland County, Virginia
October 15, 1784

Dear Madam: I set out from London the 28th of April in a post-chaise to Gravesend to meet the ship in order to set out for my own country. I remained in that town till the 30th, at which time I went on board the ship Mary Ann; we weighed anchor that instant and proceeded down the river; and the next day we passed through the Downs with a fair wind. There was no other passenger than myself, though the super-cargo was an American and a very agreeable companion.

I paid thirty guineas for my passage and expected to have had a much better stock laid in than we had, but he was a north countryman and would as soon live on salt beef and potatoes as the finest dainties in the world.

We had a passage of nine weeks, though we should have made it in a fortnight sooner had our captain run to the south and got into the trade winds, which is customary; though the reason was he had never been in America, and it was impossible for the mate or myself to persuade him from making a straight passage as he called it. He was very opinionated as to his own knowledge, though should he ever come to America again he talks of running to the southward.

Old-time Virginia barbecue

I have the pleasure of informing you, I found all my relations and friends well. I have been very happy since my arrival in Virginia; I am continually at balls and barbecues. The latter I will try to describe; it is a lamb, and sometimes a sheep, and indeed sometimes a beef, split in two and stuck on spits. A large hole is dug in the ground into which they put coals made of the bark of trees; then they lay the meat over that within about six inches of the coals; and keep basting it with butter and salt water, and turning it every now and then until it is done. We then dine sumptuously under a large shady tree or an arbour made of green bushes. We have a mile race-ground, and every horse on the field runs two and two together; by that means we have a deal of diversion; and in the evening we retire to some gentleman's house and dance awhile after supper, and then retire to bed. The company stay at the house all night (not like in your country) for every gentleman has ten or fifteen beds, which is sufficient for the ladies, and the men shift for themselves. In this manner we spend our time once a fortnight, and at other times we have regular balls as you have in England.

With the sincerest wishes for your and Mr. Cradock's health and welfare, I am, dear Madam, yours with esteem.

LAURENCE BUTLER.

Criticism Can Be a Species of Treachery

Excerpt from a letter written by THOMAS PAINE to Georges Danton,
a leader of the French Revolution
From *The Foreign Relations of the United States*
Paris, May 6, 1794 (second year of the Republic)

Citizen Danton:

As you read English, I write this letter to you without passing it through the hands of a translator. . . .

There ought to be some regulation, with respect to the spirit of denunciation that now prevails. If every individual is to indulge his private malignancy or his private ambition, to denounce at random and without any kind of proof, all confidence will be undermined and all authority be destroyed. Calumny is a species of treachery that ought to be punished as well as any other kind of treachery.

It is a private vice productive of a public evil, because it is possible to irritate men into disaffection by continual calumny, who never intended to be disaffected. It is, therefore, equally as necessary to guard against the evils of unfounded or malignant suspicion as against the evils of blind confidence. It is equally as necessary to protect the characters of public officers from calumny as it is to punish them for treachery or misconduct.

For my own part I shall hold it a matter of doubt, until better evidence arise than is known at present, whether Dumourier has been a traitor from policy or resentment. There certainly was a time when he acted well, but it is not every man whose mind is strong enough to bear up against ingratitude, and I think he experienced a great deal of this before he revolted.

Calumny becomes harmless and defeats itself when it attempts to act upon too large a scale. Thus, the denunciations of the sections against the twenty-two deputies falls to the ground. The departments that elected them are better judges of their moral and political characters than those who have denounced them. This denunciation will injure Paris in the opinion of the departments, because it has the appearance of dictating to them what sort of deputies they shall elect. Most of the acquaintance that I have in the convention are among those who are in that list, and I know there are not better men nor better patriots than what they are.

Your friend,
Thomas Paine

Compromise Makes Possible
the Impossible

From *The Federalist* by Alexander Hamilton

The zeal for attempts to amend, prior to the establishment of the constitution, must abate in every man, who is ready to accede to the truth of the following observations of a writer, equally solid and ingenious:

"To balance a large state or society, (says he,) whether monarchical or republican, on general laws, is a work of so great difficulty, that no human genius, however comprehensive, is able by the mere dint of reason and reflection, to effect it. The judgments of many must unite in the work; EXPERIENCE must guide their labour: TIME must bring it to perfection: and the FEELING of inconveniences must correct the mistakes which they *inevitably* fall into, in their first trials and experiments."*

These judicious reflections contain a lesson of moderation to all the sincere lovers of the union, and ought to put them upon their guard against hazarding anarchy, civil war, a perpetual alienation of the states from each other, and perhaps the military despotism of a victorious demagogue, in the pursuit of what they are not likely to obtain, but from TIME and EXPERIENCE.

It may be in me a defect of political fortitude, but I acknowledge that I cannot entertain an equal tranquillity with those who affect to treat the dangers of a longer continuance in our present situation as imaginary. A NATION, without a NATIONAL GOVERNMENT, is an awful spectacle. The establishment of a constitution, in time of profound peace, by the voluntary consent of a whole people, is a PRODIGY, to the completion of which

*DAVID HUME's *Essays*   · 67 ·

I look forward with trembling anxiety. In so arduous an enterprise, I can reconcile it to no rules of prudence to let go the
hold we now have, upon seven out of the thirteen states; and
after having passed over so considerable a part of the ground,
to recommence the course. I dread the more the consequences
of new attempts, because I KNOW that POWERFUL INDIVIDUALS,
in this and in other states, are enemies to a general national government in every possible shape.

Caesar Rodney's Fourth of July

by George ALFRED TOWNSEND

*A poetic version of Thomas McKean's soliloquy, as he waited
on the State House steps for the last-minute arrival of Caesar
Rodney of Delaware, whose vote made possible "The
Unanimous Declaration of the Thirteen United States."*

"Read is skulking; Dickinson is
    With conceit and fright our foeman,
Wedded to his Quaker monies,"
    Mused the grim old rebel Roman;
"Pennsylvania, spoiled by faction,
    Independence will not dare;
Maryland approves the action;
    Shall we fail on Delaware?"

In the tower the old bell rumbled,
    Striking slowly twelve o'clock.
Down the street a hot horse stumbled,
    And a man in riding frock,
With a green patch on his visage,
    And his garments white with grime.
"Now praise God!" McKean spoke grimly,
    "Caesar Rodney is on time."

Silent, hand in hand together,
    Walked they in the great square hall;
To the roll with "Aye" responded
    At the clerk's immortal call;
Listened to the Declaration
    From the steeple to the air:
"Here this day is made a nation,
    By the help of Delaware!"

Credo of a Democrat

as expressed by Thomas Jefferson to Elbridge Gerry
of Massachusetts

I am for preserving to the States the powers not yielded by
them to the Union . . . and I am not for transferring all the
powers of the States to the general government. . . .

I am for a government rigorously frugal & simple, applying
all the possible savings of the public revenue to the discharge
of the national debt; and not for a multiplication of officers
& salaries merely to make partisans, & for increasing, by every
device, the public debt, on the principle of its being a public
blessing.

I am for relying, for internal defence, on our militia solely,
till actual invasion, and for such a naval force only as may
protect our coasts and harbors from such depredations as we
have experienced; and not for a standing army in time of peace,
which may overawe the public sentiment; nor for a navy,
which, by its own expenses and the eternal wars in which
it will implicate us, will grind us with public burthens, & sink
us under them.

I am for free commerce with all nations; political connection with none; & little or no diplomatic establishment. And I am not for linking ourselves by new treaties with the quarrels of Europe; entering that field of slaughter to preserve their balance, or joining in the confederacy of kings to war against the principles of liberty.

I am for freedom of religion, & against all maneuvers to bring about a legal ascendancy of one sect over another: for freedom of the press, & against all violations of the constitution to silence by force & not by reason the complaints or criticisms, just or unjust, of our citizens against the conduct of their agents.

And I am for encouraging the progress of science in all its branches; and not for raising a hue and cry against the sacred name of philosophy; for awing the human mind by stories of raw-head & bloody bones to a distrust of its own vision, & to repose implicitly on that of others; to go backwards instead of forwards to look for improvement; to believe that government, religion, morality, & every other science were in the highest perfection in ages of the darkest ignorance, and that nothing can ever be devised more perfect than what was established by our forefathers.

To these I will add, that I was a sincere well-wisher to the success of the French revolution, and still wish it may end in the establishment of a free & well-ordered republic; but I have not been insensible under the atrocious depredations they have committed on our commerce.

The first object of my heart is my own country. In that is embarked my family, my fortune, & my own existence. I have not one farthing of interest, nor one fibre of attachment out of it, nor a single motive of preference of any one nation to another, but in proportion as they are more or less friendly to us.

An Appeal for National Unity
Thomas Jefferson's First Inaugural Address

Friends & Fellow Citizens:

Called upon to undertake the duties of the first Executive office of our country, I ... declare a sincere consciousness that the task is above my talents, & that I approach it with those anxious & awful presentiments which the greatness of the charge, & the weakness of my powers so justly inspire. . . .

All too will bear in mind this sacred principle, that though the will of the Majority is in all cases to prevail, that will to be rightful, must be reasonable: that the Minority possess their equal rights, which equal laws must protect, & to violate would be oppression.

Let us, then, fellow citizens, unite with one heart & one mind; let us restore to social intercourse that harmony & affection, without which Liberty & even Life itself, are but dreary things. And let us reflect that having banished from our land that religious intolerance under which mankind so long bled & suffered we have yet gained little if we countenance a political intolerance as despotic, as wicked & capable of as bitter & bloody persecution. . . .

But every difference of opinion, is not a difference of principle. We have called, by different names, brethren of the same principle. We are all republicans; we are all federalists. . . .

I know indeed that some honest men have feared that a republican government cannot be strong; that this government is not strong enough. But would the honest patriot, in the full tide of successful experiment abandon a government which has so far kept us free & firm on the theoretic & visionary fear that this government, the world's best hope may, by possibility, want energy to preserve itself? I trust not.

I believe this, on the contrary, the strongest government on earth. I believe it the only one where every man, at the call of the law, would fly to the standard of the law; would meet invasions of public order, as his own personal concern. Some times it is said that man cannot be trusted with the government of himself.—Can he then be trusted with the government of others? Or have we found angels in the form of kings to govern him? . . .

Let us pursue with courage & confidence our own federal and republican principles, our attachment to our Union and Representative government. Kindly separated by nature, & a wide ocean, from the exterminating havoc of one quarter of the globe . . . Possessing a chosen country, with room enough for all descendants to the 100th & 1,000th generation; Entertaining a due sense of our equal right, to the use of our own faculties, to the acquisitions of our own industry, to honor & confidence from our fellow citizens resulting not from birth, but from our actions . . . With all these blessings, what more is necessary to make us a happy and a prosperous people?

Still one thing more, fellow citizens—a wise & frugal government, which shall restrain men from injuring one another, shall leave them otherwise free to regulate their own pursuits of industry & improvement, and shall not take from the mouth of labor the bread it has earned. This is the sum of good government, & this is necessary to close the circle of our felicities.

About to enter, fellow citizens, on the exercise of duties, which comprehend everything dear & valuable to you, it is proper that you should understand what I deem the essential principle of this government, and consequently those which ought to shape its administration. I will compress them in the narrowest compass they will bear, stating the general principle. . . .

Equal & exact justice to all men, of whatever state of persuasion, religious or political:

Peace, commerce, & honest friendship with all nations, entangling alliances with none:

The support of the State governments in all their rights, as the most competent administrations for our domestic concerns, and the surest bulwarks against anti republican tendencies;

The preservation of the General government, in its whole constitutional vigor, as the sheet anchor of our peace at home, & safety abroad.

A jealous care of the right of election by the people, a mild and safe corrective of abuses, which are lopped by the sword of revolution, where peaceable remedies are unprovided.

Absolute acquiescence in the decisions of the Majority, the vital principle of republics, from which is no appeal but to force, the vital principle & immediate parent of despotism.

A well disciplined militia, our best reliance in peace, & for the first moments of war, till regulars may relieve them:

The Supremacy of the Civil over the Military authority:

Economy in public expense, that labor may be lightly burdened:

The honest payment of our debts and sacred preservation of the public faith:

Encouragement of Agriculture, & of Commerce as its handmaid:

The diffusion of information, & arraignment of all abuses at the bar of the public reason:

Freedom of Religion, freedom of the press, & freedom of Person under the protection of the Habeas corpus;

And trial by juries, impartially selected.

These Principles form the bright constellation which has gone before us, & guided our steps thro' an age of Revolution and Reformation: The wisdom of our Sages, & blood of our Heroes, have been devoted to their attainment: they should be the Creed of our political faith, the Text of civil instruction, the Touchstone by which to try the services of those we trust. . . .

And may that infinite power which rules the destinies of the universe lead our councils to what is best, and give them a favorable issue for your peace & prosperity.

He lives and will live in the memory and gratitude of the wise and good, as a luminary of science, as a votary of liberty, as a model of patriotism, and as a benefactor of human kind.

—James Madison, on the occasion of Thomas Jefferson's death, July 4, 1826, on the fiftieth anniversary of the Declaration of Independence, a document of which Jefferson was largely the author

A Legacy

by CHARLES J. BONAPARTE

From his *Address to the Yale Law School, 1890*

When, a quarter of a century since, the people of these United States had to decide the momentous question whether in North America there should be one great power, or more than one, they decided it once for all. No Roman senator or citizen echoed Cato's warning more heartily than they when they said *delenda est [must be destroyed]* of any possible competitor for supremacy on the continent. They decided then, and decided wisely, that any war, however bloody, any waste, however lavish, of life and treasure and human suffering, must be borne, if needful, that they and their children should have forever a world to themselves. And of their sacrifices we reap the just fruit; we are not perpetually thinking about fighting and getting ready to fight, only because when our fathers had fighting to do they fought to a finish.

The Marching Song
of the California Gold Rush

Written to the tune of Stephen Foster's *Oh! Susanna*,
by three passengers aboard the ship *Eliza*.

I come from Salem City,
With my washbowl on my knee;
I'm going to California,
The gold dust for to see. . . .
I jumped aboard the Liza ship,
And traveled on the sea,
And every time I thought of home
I wished it wasn't me!
The vessel reared like any horse
That had of oats a wealth,
It found it couldn't throw me,
So I thought I'd throw myself.

I thought of all the pleasant times
We've had together here;
I thought I ought to cry a bit,
But couldn't find a tear.
The pilot bread was in my mouth,
The gold dust in my eye,
And though I'm going far away,
Dear brothers, don't you cry.
I soon shall be in Francisco,
And then I'll look all round,
And when I see the gold lumps there,
I'll pick them off the ground.

I'll scrape the mountains clean, my boys,
I'll drain the rivers dry,
A pocket full of rocks bring home,
So brothers, don't you cry!
Oh, California!
That's the land for me,
I'm going to Sacramento,
With my washbowl on my knee.

First Impressions of San Francisco in 1852

by William Kelly

The houses of the city are principally built of wood, but some handsome brick edifices have lately been erected, as well as a few iron ones, and some (fewer still) of stones from the coral reefs at the Sandwich Islands; but the great scarcity of lime causes timber to be the great building staple.

The streets are regularly laid out, and are occupied, as might be expected, exclusively with warehouses and shops; some amongst which displayed the most attractive varieties of fancy goods: splendid shawls and scarfs, neat bonnets, lively dress patterns, and delicious little corsets, ingeniously arranged on stands and lines, in the spacious windows, with a skill worthy of a London artist, where that branch of business has almost attained the rank of a science. As yet, these emporiums are driving but a slender trade as compared with the other bustling marts; but every arrival augments the number of the softer sex, whose increase will serve to correct and abate many of the social evils of the city, and diversify its busy throng, who plunge from the excitement of business into that of vice, in the absence of any domestic attractions.

Hotels are numerous, but mediocre at best, and vary in their comforts and charges very considerably. At the St. Francis you get good fare and the luxury of sheets at the rate of seven dollars per day. The others slide down to twenty-one dollars per week, simplifying the fare in a proportionate ratio, and consigning you to repose in a narrow bunk, on a mattress of shavings, betwixt a pair of rough blankets, that can scarcely be included in the category of woollen manufactures; the titillation of which, superadded to the voracity of the Californian fleas, is more than a match for any amount of patience or fatigue.

There are houses of refreshment at every turn: the American Tavern, the French Restaurant, the Spanish Fonda, and the Chinese Chow-Chow. Amidst the host of competitors the Celestials carry off the palm for superior excellence in every particular. They serve everything promptly, cleanly, hot, and well cooked; they give dishes peculiar to every nation, over and above their own peculiar soups, curries, and ragouts, which cannot be even imitated elsewhere; and such are their quickness and civil attention, that they anticipate your wants, and of course secure your patronage.

VIEW OF SAN FRANCISCO (FORMERLY YERBA BUENA) IN MARCH, 1847. (AFTER A LITHOGRAPH DESIGNED AND PUBLISHED BY W. F. SWAZEY.)

There are great numbers of Chinese in California, most of whom settle in the cities. They partially adopt the prevailing costume, and constitute a very useful class of men, quick in acquiring a proficiency in the duties required of them, industrious, and persevering in attending to them; they are systematic, sober, and cleanly, and when treated with proper kindness and indulgence, become attached and interested.

They, above all others, appear successful in finding employment; for you never see a Chinese lolling about, or amongst the groups of idlers, as they are content, I believe, with more moderate wages, and unconnected with the confederate gangs, who laugh contemptuously at an offer far exceeding a colonel's pay. They soon become possessed of means, from the simplicity of their habits and the economy of their domestic ménage, and do not hesitate to share it in establishing their countrymen, who generally leave their fatherland without any other resources than their brains and sinews: a trait of character that usually affords a guarantee for other commendable attributes.

The Americans seek assiduously to inspire them with a hatred of the British, by reprobating, in terms of affected indignation, "their wanton cruelty during their unjust war;" avowing sympathies of the tenderest complexion. But those relatives of the sun and moon do not appear prone to retrospective reflections, present prospects and future anticipations more profitably and pleasingly occupying their minds.

From my experience in Sacramento, I was quite prepared for the number and style of the gaming-houses. These invariably occupy the most prominent sites; and lest their conspicuous exteriors should fail to attract the eye, a crash of music is generally heard issuing from their capacious portals and balconies, which is certain to arrest the ear. Some of them have really fine bands, as they spare no expense in securing the best musicians; and I am fully persuaded that the charm of sweet sounds entices many abhorrers of the vice to enter who would never otherwise have crossed their thresholds; but when once the Rubicon of temptation is crossed, and the turrets of gold and silver with which the tables are heaped, glitter, as they are pushed about from hand to hand, on the turn of a card or the destiny of a ball, the dazzled vision vanquishes all virtuous resolves, excites the acquisitive passions.

And those who came to scoff remain to play.

Gaming is followed, in Francisco, with a spirit accordant with its pre-eminence above the other cities of California, standing in about the same degree of comparison with the profession in Sacramento as the grand houses of aristocratic resort in St. James's and Albemarle-street do with the "silver hells" in the purlieus of Leicester-square. The Francisco gaming-houses are never closed, morning, noon, or night. Dealers and presidents succeed each other; and as yawning crowds disperse at daybreak, new victims rush from their beds to the sacrifice, so that there is no intermission, the only difference being that the evening attendance is the greatest and most adventurous.

There are various games, adapted to every prejudice and caprice; but *the* game is *monté*. It is on this that all large investments are made, and this which leviathan gamblers patronise. I was myself present on one occasion when a gentleman lost six thousand dollars at three stakes. It is, however, remarked, by those qualified to pronounce statistically, that while the numbers who resort to those "hells" are undiminished, the amounts played for are fast dwindling in magnitude. This is a consequence not to be wondered at; for communities cannot, any more than bodies corporeal, bear up against bleeding beyond a certain point without syncope ensuing; and some conception of the Francisco drainage by gambling may be formed, when it is known that one establishment, the El Dorado, can afford to pay a rent of six thousand dollars per month, independent of taxes and expenses: a revenue enabling its proprietors to indulge in the most expensive style of living, and to set aside enormous sums for other speculative investments.

* * *

Persons above all temptation, who find time hanging heavily on their hands, can beguile an hour or two in the different law courts, where justice is administered in a manner that comes home to the meanest capacity, divested of all that stupid etiquette and solemn decorum so irksome according to British discipline.

Francisco judges sit on the bench attired like other men, and, taking a leaf out of Chief Baron Nicholson's book, puff their cigars while laying down the law, on the enlightened principle of *"ex fumo, dare lucem."* Nor do they haughtily hesitate to accommodate with the glowing butt any of the learned counsel or audience who may require a light: in fact, there is a degree of charming republican familiarity existing between the bench, the bar, and the public, which makes a man feel as much at ease in court as in a tavern, and must be seen to be properly appreciated. Law arguments under such a system are no longer dry and uninteresting, but flow smoothly along, liberally lubricated with tobacco juice, and garnished with colloquial episodes that come with a delicious freshness upon the ear of a person only accustomed to the oppressive profundity of Westminster practice.

I was being thus edified, sitting in the jury-box (no jury being empanelled at the time), where I observed a row of new pine sticks, each about the dimensions of a shillelagh, standing in exact order in front of the seats; and finding their number amounting precisely to twelve, it struck me they were part of the legal machinery of the place. I was not astray; for a sort of factotum—crier, usher, tipstaff &c.—who wore his hat ex officio, commiseratingly informed me they were "desk protectors," which it was part of his duty as court-keeper to provide as "whittling stuff for the gents," who would otherwise cut all sorts of hieroglyphics and incongruous devices upon the desks: an operation I afterwards saw gone through by a witness under the ordeal of a sharp cross-examination, who cut with an increasing keenness into the rail as the counsel cut into his credibility.

AMERICANA
as It Developed Along the Mail Routes

From *The Story of Our Post Office* by MARSHALL CUSHING

John Barner reached Bloomington, Indiana, the site of the State University, in 1828. He used to say:

There was then a mail route from Louisville, Kentucky, through New Albany, Salem, Bedford, Bloomington, Martinsville, the Bluffs of White River, to Indianapolis, the seat of government. The mail was carried on horseback by Colonel Green, once a week, and on nearing the towns he would sound his long tin trumpet to announce to the citizens the arrival of the United States mail "on horseback."

There was a mail route from Madison through Columbus and Franklin to Indianapolis—one from Cincinnati, via Lawrenceburg, Greensburg and Shelbyville to Indianapolis—and a route from Cincinnati via Oxford, Liberty, Connersville and Rushville to the state capital. I think, as early as 1830, a stage was run on this route by John Lister, one among the first contractors for coach service in the state.

The Cumberland or National Road, from the east through Columbus—Richmond, Indianapolis and Terre Haute, Indiana —Springfield, Illinois, and Jefferson City, Missouri, was "cut out," large trees removed, and the center grubbed in 1828, 1829, 1830 and 1831. Through Indianapolis on west, the mails were first carried on this road on horseback, and frequently detained for a week on account of high water—no bridges at that date. Stages and wagons got through the deep soil, as far back as 1842, on this road by prying out the wheels at the deepest mud holes.

The Michigan Road was surveyed and marked from Lake Michigan through Logansport, by act of the State Legislature, approved in January, 1828, under a treaty made with the Miami Indians for the lands with which to construct the road. This road was from Madison, Indiana, to the lake. It became a mail route, and the mail was carried on horseback from the state capital north to the lake in 1833. A portion of this route was through swamps, and had to be traveled around to shun the impassable obstructions. After coaches, or stages, were put on the route, from about 1836 to 1852, passengers starting in the coaches were compelled to get out and carry a fence rail

to pry the wheels of the vehicle out of the many mud holes on the road. Horses frequently sank to midsides in water and mud.

The first mail was carried on horseback from Lafayette via Jefferson four miles west, to Frankfort, twenty-four miles east of Lafayette, in the year 1830. The county seat was located and lots sold July 12, 1830. Colonel Samuel D. Maxwell was the first postmaster and first county clerk—a gentleman of fine culture and one among the best citizens and pioneers. He was afterward mayor of Indianapolis.

The first mail I saw arrive in the city was in April, 1832, the year I settled here. The "post boy," a young man, John Ross, carried it from Lafayette to Jefferson on horseback, and then on foot to Frankfort, four miles, in a small pouch like an old pair of saddle-bags.

I was appointed postmaster at this place in February, 1834, to succeed the first postmaster. I was then a poor young man, a mechanic, with a small family, and was well pleased with the position, as I thought it might bring a little revenue—about $30 per quarter. The first mail I opened was on the 3rd day of February, 1834. Jerry Dunn, the "post boy," reached the western suburbs of the town and tooted aloud his tin horn.

Sometimes a new citizen residing near the principal stream, Sugar Creek, would send the carrier back with a note reading as follows: "From my knowledge of Sugar Creek, the mail cannot pass over with safety," signed by Joseph Wood. Consequently, we were without a mail for two weeks.

In 1838, 1839, and 1840, a four-horse coach was put on a "new route," as it was called, from Indianapolis north on the Michigan Road via Kirklin, Frankfort, Jefferson and Huntersville to Lafayette. This line of stages ran daily between the points named.

It generally took day and night to run the sixty-five miles. The coaches were well loaded with passengers from the east "going west." Daniel Hunter, the contractor, finally failed, and the coaches were taken off the line.

In 1848, Jacob Jones put coaches on the line from Indianapolis via Kirklin, Frankfort and Rossville to Delphi. He and Andrew McIntyre continued to run the coaches or light wagons three times a week till 1854. About that time the Indianapolis and Lafayette Railroad was completed to Lafayette and we were supplied with a daily mail, from Colfax Station to Frankfort, ten miles, by coaches over a swampy, "bad," mud road.

In October, 1838, Amos Kendall, Postmaster General, passed through Indianapolis on a tour of inspection of the service, I suppose. A short time afterward he started an "express" or "fast mail," from Washington or Baltimore west on the National Road to St. Louis or Jefferson City.

In February, 1839, I saw one of the mail boys riding his horse in a lope on that road between Richmond and Indianapolis. I think he changed horses every forty or fifty miles, and carried a small mail sack. The experiment was soon abandoned.

The post office furniture in the Frankfort office from 1831 to 1841 consisted of a table, twenty-nine by thirty-six inches, with a drawer made underneath; an alphabet case of twenty-six for letters, and the same number for newspapers, placed one above the other on the back of the table.

I could generally tell who had mail matter in the office, but many times went to the boxes to satisfy persons who thought differently. I was once twenty-four miles from home in a neighboring town, and a patron of the office made his way through a large gathering of people and asked me if there was a letter in the office for him.

The Short-lived Presidency of Martin Van Buren

From *The Fabulous Forties, 1840–1850* by MEADE MINNIGERODE
Copyright, 1924, by Meade Minnigerode
Published by G. P. Putnam's Sons

M r. Van Buren only carried seven States. The bewildered, and bitterly indignant, Democratic press wailed its loud misgivings over all this hornswogglery in gloomy, and not altogether unjustified, terms. The only hope was that the political buffoonery of 1840 would ever stand, solitary and alone, on the page of history, a damning stain on the brow of Federalism. No more might the world see coons, cabins and cider usurp the place of principles, nor doggerel verse elicit a shout while reason was passed by with a sneer.

"We have been sung down, lied down, drunk down!" So, dismally, they summed it up.

The Whig press, on the other hand, gave utterance to triumphantly sanctimonious outcries, the burden of which was that the people were free once more, that the election was a victory of principle over power, of liberty over despotism, of right and justice over wrong and oppression, of prosperity and happiness over widespread ruin and desolation. In short, that, to put it mildly——

"A great people have placed their seal of condemnation upon a band of the most desperate, aspiring, and unprincipled demagogues that ever graced the annals of despotism, a band of bold and reckless innovators calling themselves the democracy of the land, at whose head was Martin Van Buren, a monarchist in principle, a tyrant and a despot in practice."

They had such a pleasant polemic style in the Forties!

In the midst of the commotion the Philadelphia *Public Ledger,* for its part, sourly observed that: "millions of dollars will now change hands on election bets, millions of days have been taken from useful labor to listen to stump orators, and millions more to build log cabins, erect hickory poles, and march in ridiculous, degrading, mob creating processions; millions of dollars have been wasted in soul and body destroying intemperance, in paying demagogues for preaching treason and bribing knaves to commit perjury and cast fraudulent votes. However high the hopes inspired by the election of General Harrison, they will prove to be delusive."

And so they did, but not precisely in the manner anticipated. The new president was inaugurated on March 4, 1841, during the course of which ceremony he made a long speech—but not as long as it had been before Mr. Clay ran his blue pencil through it—full of allusions to Rome, to Greece, to the Swiss Republic even, and with never a reference to any of the issues of the day. One month later he was dead.

To Autumn

Season of mists and mellow fruitfulness,
  Close bosom-friend of the maturing sun;
Conspiring with him how to load and bless
  With fruit the vines that round the thatch-eves run;
To bend with apples the moss'd cottage-trees,
  And fill all fruit with ripeness to the core;
    To swell the gourd, and plump the hazel shells
With a sweet kernel; to set budding more,
  And still more, later flowers for the bees,
  Until they think warm days will never cease,
    For Summer has o'er-brimmed their clammy cells.

Who hath not seen thee oft amid thy store?
  Sometimes whoever seeks abroad may find
Thee sitting careless on a granary floor,
  Thy hair soft-lifted by the winnowing wind;
Or on a half-reap'd furrow sound asleep,
  Drows'd with the fume of poppies, while thy hook
    Spares the next swath and all its twined flowers:
And sometimes like a gleaner thou dost keep
  Steady thy laden head across a brook;
  Or by a cyder-press, with patient look,
    Thou watchest the last oozings hours by hours.

Where are the songs of Spring? Ay, where are they?
  Think not of them, thou hast thy music too,—
While barred clouds bloom the soft-dying day,
  And touch the stubble-plains with rosy hue;
Then in a wailful choir the small gnats mourn
  Among the river swallows, borne aloft
    Or sinking as the light wind lives or dies;
And full-grown lambs loud bleat from hilly bourn;
  Hedge-crickets sing; and now with treble soft
  The red-breast whistles from a garden-croft;
    And gathering swallows twitter in the skies.

by JOHN KEATS

A Close Call with a Large Bear

by WILLIAM KELLY

I now took a long farewell of the horses, and turned north-ward, selecting a line close in by the base of the hills, going along at an improved pace, with a view of reaching the trading-post the same night; but stopping in a gully to look for water, I found a little pool, evidently scratched out by a bear, as there were footprints and claw-marks about it; and I was aware that instinct prompts that brute, where water is nearest the surface, to scratch until he comes to it.

This had been one of very large size, the footmark behind the toes being fully nine inches long; and although I had my misgivings about the prudence of a tête-á-tête with a great grizzly bear, still the "better part of valour" was overcome, as it often is, by the anticipated honour and glory of a single combat, and the conquest of such a formidable beast. I was well armed, too, with my favourite rifle, a Colt's revolver, which had never disappointed me, and a nondescript weapon, a sort of cross betwixt a claymore and a bowie-knife. After capping afresh, hanging the bridle on the horn of the saddle, and stak-ing my mule, I followed the trail up a gully, and much sooner than I expected came within view and good shooting distance of Bruin, who was seated erect, with his side towards me, in front of a manzanita bush, making a repast on his favourite berry.

The sharp click of the cock, causing him to turn quickly round, left little time for deliberation; so, taking a prompt and steady aim at the region of the heart, I let drive. The ball, as I subsequently found, glanced along the ribs, entering under the shoulder, and shattering some of the bones. I exulted as I saw him stagger and fall upon his side. The next glance, however, revealed him, to my dismay, on all-fours, in direct pursuit, but going lame; so I bolted for the mule, sadly encum-bered with a huge pair of Mexican spurs, the noise of the crashing brush close in my rear convincing me that he was fast gaining on me. I therefore dropped my rifle, putting on fresh steam, and reaching the rope, pulled up the picket-pin, and, springing into the saddle with merely a hold of the lariat, plunged the spurs into the mule, which action, much to my affright, produced a kick and a retrograde movement. In the exertion, having got a glimpse of my pursuer, he uttered a snort of terror, and went off at a pace I did not think him

capable of, soon widening the distance betwixt us and the bear; but having no means of guiding his motions, he brought me violently in contact with the arm of a tree, which unhorsed and stunned me exceedingly.

Scrambling to my feet as well as I could, I saw my relentless enemy close at hand, leaving me only the alternative of ascending a tree; but, in my hurried and nervous efforts, I had scarcely my feet above his reach when he was right under, evidently enfeebled by the loss of blood, as his struggles made it well out copiously. After a moment's pause, and a fierce glance upwards from his bloodshot eyes, he clasped the trunk; but I saw that his endeavours to climb were crippled by the wounded shoulder. However, by the aid of his jaws, he succeeded in reaching the first branch with his sound arm, and was working convulsively to bring up the body, when, with a well-directed blow from my cutlass, I completely severed the tendons of the foot, and he instantly fell, with a dreadful souse and horrific growl, the blood spouting up as if impelled from a jet. He rose again somewhat tardily, and limping round the tree with upturned eyes, kept tearing off the bark with his tusks. Watching my opportunity, and leaning downwards, I sent a ball from my revolver with such good effect immediately behind the head, that he dropped; and my nerves being now rather more composed, I leisurely distributed the remaining five balls in the most vulnerable parts of his carcass.

By this time I saw the muscular system totally relaxed, so I descended with confidence, and found him quite dead, and myself not a little enervated with the excitement and the effects of my wound on the temple, which bled profusely; so much so, that I thought an artery was ruptured. I bound up my head as well as I could, loaded my revolver anew, and returned for my rifle; but as evening was approaching, and my mule gone, I had little time to survey the dimensions of my fallen foe, and no means of packing much of his flesh. I therefore hastily hacked off a few steaks from his thigh, and hewing off one of his hind-feet as a trophy of victory, I set out towards the trading-post, which I reached about midnight, my friend and my truant mule being there before me, but no horses.

I exhibited the foot of my late antagonist in great triumph, and described the conflict with due emphasis and effect to the company, who rose to listen; after which I made a transfer of the flesh to the traders, on condition that there was not to be any charge for the hotel or the use of the mule.

There was an old and experienced French trapper of the party, who, judging from the size of the foot, set down the weight of the bear at fifteen hundred pounds, which, he said, they frequently exceed, he himself, as well as Colonel Fremont's exploring party, having killed several that weighed two thousand pounds. He advised me, should I again be pursued by a bear, and have no other means of escape, to ascend a small-girthed tree, which they cannot get up; for, not having any central joint in the fore-legs, they cannot climb any with a branchless stem that does not fully fill their embrace; and in the event of not being able to accomplish the ascent before my pursuer overtook me, to place my back against the tree, when, if it and I did not constitute a bulk capable of filling his hug, I might have time to rip out his entrails before he could kill me, being in a most favourable posture for the operation.

Bears do not generally use their mouths in the destruction of their victims, but, hugging them closely, lift one of the hind-feet, which are armed with tremendous claws, and tear out the bowels. The Frenchman's advice reads rationally enough, and is a feasible theory of the art of evading ursine compression; but, unfortunately, in the haunts of the animal those slim juvenile saplings are rarely met with, and a person closely confronted with such a savage vis-à-vis is not exactly in a tone of nerve for surgical operations.

After the Election
the President Represents All the People

Above all things, the function of a minority party is educational in character. It will not do for the great rank and file of the American people to be intensely interested in the issues and party programs for a couple of months before election and then permit that interest to die out when the result is announced. Political platforms and political promises are not self-enacting. The political history of the United States clearly indicates that every progressive step, every great governmental reform has been won only after a period of persistent effort and by the slow process of educating the electorate.

The first and indispensable element of education is information. A full and complete presentation of the facts. That is easier to do today than it was years ago, with the use of the radio and the increasing interest of our young people in public affairs. It must be remembered that while political parties may seriously divide public opinion throughout the country during the progress of a campaign, after the American people have made their decision the man selected is not the President of the Republican Party, but is the President of the United States. He is the President of all the people and as such he is entitled to the cooperation of every citizen in the development of a program calculated to promote the welfare and best interests of this country. He is entitled to a fair opportunity to develop such a program. Only when he fails to accomplish it does the administration become the subject of proper criticism by the opposition party.

Premature criticism not only fails of its purpose, but often results to the disadvantage of the critic himself. Party responsibility is not confined to its handling of governmental affairs. A political party must also be accountable to the people of the United States for the management of its internal affairs, and no political party can afford to accept the support of forces for which it refuses to accept responsibility. It will not do to let bitterness, rancor or indignation over the result blind us to the one outstanding fact, that above everything else we are Americans.

No matter with what party we align ourselves on election day, our concern should be for the future welfare, happiness, content and prosperity of the American people.

From Alfred E. Smith's Post-Election Radio Address
New York City, November 13, 1928

What Is True Patriotism?

by Sydney J. Harris

From *Strictly Personal*, his column in the *Chicago Daily News*

Courtesy *Chicago Daily News* and Publishers-Hall Syndicate

Most people fail to understand the difference between "patriotism" and "nationalism."

Patriotism is wanting what is best for your country. Nationalism is thinking your country is best, no matter what it does.

Patriotism means asking your country to conform to the highest laws of man's nature, to the eternal standards of justice and equality. Nationalism means supporting your country even when it violates these eternal standards.

Patriotism means going underground if you have to—as the anti-Nazis in Germany did—and working for the overthrow of your government when it becomes evil and inhuman and incapable of reform.

Nationalism means "going along" with a Hitler or a Stalin or any other tyrant who waves the flag, mouths obscene devotion to the Fatherland, and meanwhile tramples the rights of people.

Patriotism is a form of faith. Nationalism is a form of superstition, of fanaticism, of idolatry.

Patriotism would like every country to become like ours, in its best aspects. Nationalism despises other countries as incapable of becoming like ours.

Just as we fail to understand the difference between patriotism and nationalism, so many people fail to understand what "Americanism" really consists of.

"Americanism" was something utterly new in the world when it was conceived by our Founding Fathers. It was not just another form of nationalism—indeed, it was a repudiation of all the then existing nationalisms

It was conceived as a form of government, unrestricted to one geographical place or one kind of people It was open to all men everywhere—no matter where they were born or came from. In this respect, it was utterly unique. Its patriotism was potentially world-wide.

The word "Americanism" must not be narrowed or flattened or coarsened to apply to one flag, one people, one government. In its highest, original sense, it asks that all men become patriots *to an idea*, not to a particular country or government. And this idea is self-government by all men, who are regarded as equals in the law.

This is why American patriotism—properly understood—is the best patriotism in the world, because it is for all the world, and not just for us. To confuse it with nationalism, to use it for ugly purposes, is to betray the dream of those who made it come true.

★ ★ ★ ★ ★ ★ ★ ★ ★ ★ ★ ★ ★

Defeat and Victory

by WALLACE RICE

From *American History by American Poets*
Edited by Nellie Urner Wallington
Copyright, 1911, by Duffield & Company

Through the clangor of the cannon,
  Through the combat's wreck and reek,
Answer to th' o'ermastering *Shannon*
  Thunders from the *Chesapeake;*
Gallant Lawrence, wounded, dying,
  Speaks with still unconquered lip
    Ere the bitter draught he drinks:—
Keep the Flag flying!
  Fight her till she strikes or sinks!
Don't give up the ship!

Still that voice is sounding o'er us,
  So bold Perry heard it call;
Farragut has joined its chorus;
  Porter, Dewey, Wainwright—all
Heard the voice of duty crying;
  Deathless word from dauntless lip
    That our past and future links:—
Keep the Flag flying!
  Fight her till she strikes or sinks!
Don't give up the ship!

★ ★ ★ ★ ★ ★ ★ ★ ★ ★ ★ ★ ★

Dissidents in His Own Party
Wanted to Defeat Lincoln in 1864

From an essay by CARL SCHURZ

The differences of opinion concerning the subject of recon-
struction had only intensified the feeling against Lincoln which
had long been nursed among the radicals, and some of them
openly declared their purpose of resisting his reelection to the
presidency. Similar sentiments were manifested by the advanced anti-slavery men of Missouri, who, in their hot faction-
fight with the "conservatives" of that State, had not received
from Lincoln the active support they demanded.

Still another class of Union men, mainly in the East, gravely
shook their heads when considering the question whether
Lincoln should be reelected. They were those who cherished
in their minds an ideal of statesmanship and of personal bearing
in high office with which, in their opinion, Lincoln's individuality was much out of accord. They were shocked when they
heard him cap an argument upon grave affairs of state with a
story about "a man out in Sangamon County,"—a story, to be
sure, strikingly clinching his point, but sadly lacking in dignity.
They could not understand the man who was capable, in opening a cabinet meeting, of reading to his secretaries a funny
chapter from a recent book of Artemus Ward, with which in
an unoccupied moment he had relieved his care-burdened mind,
and who then solemnly informed the executive council that he
had vowed in his heart to issue a proclamation emancipating
the slaves as soon as God blessed the Union arms with another
victory. They were alarmed at the weakness of a President
who would indeed resist the urgent remonstrances of statesmen against his policy, but could not resist the prayer of an
old woman for the pardon of a soldier who was sentenced to
be shot for desertion.

Such men, mostly sincere and ardent patriots, not only
wished, but earnestly set to work, to prevent Lincoln's renomination. Not a few of them actually believed, in 1863, that, if
the national convention of the Union party were held then,
Lincoln would not be supported by the delegation of a single
State. But when the convention met at Baltimore, in June, 1864,
the voice of the people was heard. On the first ballot Lincoln
received the votes of the delegations from all the States except
Missouri; and even the Missourians turned over their votes to

LINCOLN AND HIS SON "TAD."

him before the result of the ballot was declared.

But even after his renomination the opposition to Lincoln within the ranks of the Union party did not subside. A convention, called by the dissatisfied radicals in Missouri, and favored by men of a similar way of thinking in other States, had been held already in May, and had nominated as its candidate for the presidency General Frémont. He, indeed, did not attract a strong following, but opposition movements from different quarters appeared more formidable. Henry Winter Davis and Benjamin Wade assailed Lincoln in a flaming manifesto. Other Union men, of undoubted patriotism and high standing, persuaded themselves, and sought to persuade the people, that Lincoln's renomination was ill advised and dangerous to the Union cause. As the Democrats had put off their convention until the 29th of August, the Union party had, during the larger part of the summer, no opposing candidate and platform to attack, and the political campaign languished.

Neither were the tidings from the theatre of war of a cheering character. The terrible losses suffered by Grant's army in the battles of the Wilderness spread general gloom. Sherman seemed for a while to be in a precarious position before Atlanta. The opposition to Lincoln within the Union party grew louder in its complaints and discouraging predictions. Earnest demands were heard that his candidacy should be withdrawn. Lincoln himself, not knowing how strongly the masses were attached to him, was haunted by dark forebodings of defeat.

Then the scene suddenly changed as if by magic. The Democrats, in their national convention, declared the war a failure, demanded, substantially, peace at any price, and nominated on such a platform General McClellan as their candidate. Their convention had hardly adjourned when the capture of Atlanta gave a new aspect to the military situation. It was like a sun-ray bursting through a dark cloud. The rank and file of the Union party rose with rapidly growing enthusiasm. The song "We are coming, Father Abraham, three hundred thousand strong," resounded all over the land. Long before the decisive day arrived, the result was beyond doubt, and Lincoln was reelected President by overwhelming majorities.

The election over, even his severest critics found themselves forced to admit that Lincoln was the only possible candidate for the Union party in 1864, and that neither political combinations nor campaign speeches, nor even victories in the field, were needed to insure his success. The plain people had all the while been satisfied with Abraham Lincoln: they confided in him; they loved him; they felt themselves near to him; they saw personified in him the cause of Union and freedom; and they went to the ballot-box for him in their strength.

The hour of triumph called out the characteristic impulses of his nature. The opposition within the Union party had stung him to the quick. Now he had his opponents before him, baffled and humiliated. Not a moment did he lose to stretch out the hand of friendship to all.

"Now that the election is over," he said, in response to a serenade, "may not all, having a common interest, reunite in a common effort to save our common country? For my own part, I have striven, and will strive, to place no obstacle in the way. So long as I have been here I have not willingly planted a thorn in any man's bosom. While I am deeply sensible to the high compliment of a reelection, it adds nothing to my satisfaction that any other man may be pained or disappointed by the result. May I ask those who were with me to join with me in the same spirit toward those who were against me?"

This was Abraham Lincoln's character as tested in the furnace of prosperity.

Exciting Early Experiences in the U.S. Postal Department

as narrated by William H. Wallace of Hammondsville, Ohio

From *The Story of Our Post Office* by MARSHALL CUSHING

I have travelled in the stage when it took three days and three nights to reach Philadelphia from Pittsburgh. One newspaper of small dimensions in the county town for the whole county was a rule, and many in the county never scanned its columns; and if they did, the general or far off news did not come under their eye. Then farmers and farmers' sons were dubbed clodhoppers. Ask them the governor's name and they could not tell it. I know of families of some prominence in the county when I was a boy, that never saw a newspaper.

Just seventy-three years ago [1819] in the city of Baltimore, I witnessed the hanging, for robbing the United States mail, of the noted Haire and his co-worker, then the greatest robbers of mails. Then it was a death penalty to rob the United States mail.

Shortly after was another hanging in the same city that I witnessed. Hutton and Hull robbed the mail not far out of the city, and murdered the driver, Heaps. Heaps and his family lived in the city, and his children were my playmates. There were no express lines, the mails being the only public mode to send money. The villains stopped the mail coach in the night with none but the driver aboard. He was ordered to give up the mail. This he did; but it was concluded, fearing detection and arrest, to take the driver's life by shooting and stabbing, each taking a hand. They then tied the two horses by the lines to a tree, and made off with the mail.

They visited the city next day and were arrested. Hutton was an old offender, and young Hull inveighed as an accomplice. He was only about twenty years old; had studied medicine in Utica where his father, who was a druggist, lived.

My first trip on business to Philadelphia was sixty-one years ago [1831] by mail stage, and I returned home via the Baltimore and Ohio Railroad as far as it was built. The road was made to Ellicott's Mills, thirteen miles, with strap rail; two horses tandem; capacity of coach twelve or fifteen; rate of speed ten miles per hour. This mode was continued until finished to Frederick, when I was again a passenger; next, pony-sized locomotives from Baltimore to Cumberland, thence by mail stage to Brownsville, Pennsylvania.

I crossed the Alleghenies twenty-six times before the railroad traversed them. The robbery of the mails while en route by stage was common, and for safety at times postilions were brought into requisition. The common way of carrying money by person was to encase it in a leathern belt, or silk bandanna handkerchief, placing that around the body next to the bare hide.

My first trip over the Alleghenies from Baltimore to Brownsville was in the month of August, 1820, just seventy-two years ago the past August, in my bare head and bare feet. The sun was hot, and so was the pike road.

On March 4, 1829, General Jackson succeeded Mr. Adams as President, and the way the Postmaster General, John McLean, and the postmasters of any note had to fly the track, was a caution. "To the victors belong the spoils" was the ruling motto.

I visited Washington fifty-eight years ago; was formally introduced to General Jackson at the White House by a member of Congress, and had a good little talk. He held in his hand a two-cent clay pipe, which he had been smoking. I also had a good talk with Henry Clay. One day when the House was not in session my member of Congress seated me on the speaker's chair, saying, "Now you can say that you have sat in the speaker's chair."

Neither Philadelphia nor New York was flooded then with periodicals. No *Tribune*, no *Herald*, no *Times*, no *Ledger*. In regard to men of great wealth, they did not flourish, leaving out Stephen Girard. The Ridgeways were spoken of; Cornelius Vanderbilt of New York was then taking in pennies for ferrying with his skiff, ferrying in his teens; John Jacob Astor and his wife cleaned and prepared furs, and she said they must wait till they would get ahead before they could afford to eat a cooky.

Large hotels did not abound in either city. Nearly fifty years ago the Washington House on Chestnut Street was opened. On my arrival in Philadelphia in the morning, after a three days' and three nights' stage ride from Pittsburgh, a friend said to me, "A new hotel has just opened on Chestnut Street; try that for a change." I accordingly repaired to the place, entered my name, etc. When dinner was anounced, I entered the dining room and there was a most sumptuous repast, and a corps of caparisoned waiters. But behold, not a solitary guest besides myself! And all the waiters wanted to take a hand at serving me. It was really a strange ordeal to pass through, but I finally came out all right.

Naming the Republican Party

From *History of the Republican Party in Illinois*
Copyright 1912, by C. A. Church

The selection of the name "Republican" for the new uprising was a matter of development rather than any definite and formal christening. "Seven cities fought for Homer dead." Many cities have likewise claimed the distinction of giving the Republican party its "start in the world." Great movements are in the air in any marked period of transition. No man or city can exclusively claim them. They are rather the result of the awakened conscience of a people. From this fact arises the difficulty, if not impossibility, of determining the birthplace of this great American party of freedom.

There are, however, certain facts that have been established with reasonable certainty concerning the origin of the name. Henry Wilson, former vice-president of the United States, in his "Rise and Fall of the Slave-Power," is authority for the statement that on the night following the final passage of the Kansas-Nebraska act, a meeting of senators and representatives in congress who had opposed that measure indorsed the plan for such an organization. At an anti-Nebraska meeting in Ripon, Wisconsin, March 29, 1854, Alvin E. Bovay suggested the name Republican for the new party. It is now generally conceded that Michigan took the lead in formally adopting the name Republican at a state convention held at Jackson, July 6, 1854. In 1904, on the fiftieth anniversary of that event, President Roosevelt declined the honor of an invitation to be present on the ground that the birthplace of the party was a matter of dispute, and that he did not wish to give official recognition to any of the rival claimants.

Wisconsin followed Michigan, July 13, and Vermont, at a state convention the same day, selected the name Republican. It was adopted in Massachusetts at a mass meeting July 20. In Illinois there was hesitancy among the anti-Nebraska leaders, and it required some time to overcome this prejudice and acquiesce in the action of neighboring states. The anti-Nebraska convention, held at Springfield in October, 1854, which will be subsequently considered, adopted a platform in harmony with what afterward became the principles of the Republican party. The name, however, was not adopted, although Mr. Lincoln, in a letter to Ichabod Codding, referred to "the Republican party."

George Washington Explains His Devotion to Duty and Responsibility

Gentlemen,

In every act of my administration I have sought the happiness of my fellow citizens. My system for the attainment of this object has uniformly been to overlook all personal, local, and partial considerations; to contemplate the United States as one great whole; to consider that sudden impressions, when erroneous, would yield to candid reflection; and to consult only the substantial and permanent interests of our country.

Nor have I departed from this line of conduct on the occasion which has produced the resolutions contained in your letter of the 13th.

Without a predilection for my own judgment, I have weighed with attention every argument which has at any time been brought into view. But the Constitution is the guide which I never can abandon. It has assigned to the President the power of making treaties, with the advice and consent of the Senate. It was doubtless supposed that these two branches of government would combine, without passion and with the best means of information, those facts and principles upon which the success of our foreign relations will always depend; that they ought not to substitute for their own conviction the opinions of others; or to seek truth through any channel but that of a temperate and well informed investigation.

Under this persuasion, I have resolved on the manner of executing the duty before me. To the high responsibility attached to it, I freely submit, and you, gentlemen, are at liberty to make these sentiments known as the grounds of my procedure. While I feel the most lively gratitude for the many instances of approbation from my country, I can no otherwise deserve it than by obeying the dictates of my conscience.

With due respect,
I am, gentlemen,
Your obedient

28th July, 1795   George Washington

⋮

Thoughts on the Shape of the Human Body

by Rupert Brooke

How can we find? how can we rest? how can
We, being gods, win joy, or peace, being man?
We, the gaunt zanies of a witless Fate,
Who love the unloving and lover hate,
Forget the moment ere the moment slips,
Kiss with blind lips that seek beyond the lips,
Who want, and know not what we want, and cry
With crooked mouths for Heaven, and throw it by.
Love's for completeness! No perfection grows
'Twixt leg, and arm, elbow, and ear, and nose,
And joint, and socket; but unsatisfied
Sprawling desires, shapeless, perverse, denied.
Finger with finger wreathes; we love, and gape,
Fantastic shape to mazed fantastic shape,
Straggling, irregular, perplexed, embossed,
Grotesquely twined, extravagantly lost
By crescive paths and strange protuberant ways
From sanity and from wholeness and from grace.
How can love triumph, how can solace be,
Where fever turns toward fever, knee toward knee?
Could we but fill to harmony, and dwell
Simple as our thought and as perfectible,
Rise disentangled from humanity
Strange whole and new into simplicity,
Grow to a radiant round love, and bear
Unfluctuant passion for some perfect sphere,
Love moon to moon unquestioning, and be
Like the star Lunisequa, steadfastly
Following the round clear orb of her delight,
Patiently ever, through the eternal night!

⋮

The Role of the Female

From *The Fabulous Forties, 1840-1850* by MEADE MINNIGERODE
Copyright, 1924, by Meade Minnigerode
Published by G. P. Putnam's Sons

They had discovered, already in 1842, that: "the great misfortune that lies in the path of highly cultivated women is
the absence of active occupation for their mental energy....
Men have professions and offices; to them belong, by right
of courtesy, all the activities and authorities of life. Author-
ship is the only accredited seat for a woman's intellect; and
this, by obviating one evil, induces many others. The fever
of unoccupied energy is quenched, but by and by the worse
fever of sensitive ambition arises....

"Where must the cure be sought?" the essayist asked. "In
an inconceivably higher education of what may be called the
sense of responsibility. Wherever genius indisputably exists
in a girl, there let parents frankly acknowledge its existence,
and on that admission ground a simple but serious inculcation
of these doctrines—that to possess intellect is an accident, not
a merit; that it is by no means a novelty... and that superior
knowledge is worthless without active virtue. Parents must
learn to regard as nothing short of sin all efforts to stimulate
a girl's mind for the gratification either of their vanity or
hers....

"The gifted girl feels man has taken the birthright and she
fancies that for her, no blessings are left. The grand fact is that
in most of the triumphs achieved by men she has shared in the
purest form by having been their instructor, instigator or
friend. Separate and individual triumphs are the lot of few
women, and those few are rarely truly happy for them; but
collateral triumphs she may have without number. How few
have been the distinguished men who have not acknowl-
edged that their deepest obligations have been to a wife, a
sister, or, above all, a mother! Let the mind of every girl,
especially of every girl of talent, be sedulously directed to
this cheering view of female influence—to the beautiful and
refreshing undercurrent which it may furnish in the troubled
course of daily life....

"As a general hint there was much wisdom in the advice
given by an old mother to a young one: Stimulate the sen-
sibilities of your boys, and blunt those of your girls."

The Art and Pleasure of a Well-Planned Dinner

From *The Complete Works of Montaigne*, translated by DONALD M. FRAME

There is jealousy and envy between our pleasures; they clash and interfere with each other.

Alcibiades, a connoisseur in making good cheer, banished even music from the table, so that it should not disturb the pleasure of conversation, for the reason that Plato ascribes to him, that it is a practice of vulgar men to call in instrumentalists and singers to their feasts, for lack of the good talk and enjoyable remarks with which intelligent men know how to entertain each other.

Varro asks this of a banquet: a gathering of people of handsome presence and agreeable conversation, who are neither mute nor garrulous; cleanliness and delicacy in the food and the place; and fair weather.

A well-planned dinner takes more than a little art and gives more than a little pleasure; neither the great generals nor the great philosophers have spurned the practice and science of it. My imagination has entrusted three dinners to the keeping of my memory, which fortune rendered outstandingly pleasant to me at different times in my more flourishing days. For each of the guests himself brings the principal charm, according to the good temper of body and soul in which he happens to be. My present condition excludes me from this.

I, who operate only close to the ground, hate that inhuman wisdom that would make us disdainful enemies of the cultivation of the body. I consider it equal injustice to set our heart against natural pleasures and to set our heart too much on them. Xerxes was a fool, who, wrapped in all human pleasures, went and offered a prize to anyone who would find him others. But hardly less of a fool is the man who cuts off those that nature has found for him.

We should neither pursue them nor flee them, we should accept them. I accept them with more gusto and with better grace than most, and more willingly let myself follow a natural inclination.

We have no need to exaggerate their inanity; it makes itself felt enough and evident enough. Much thanks to our sickly, kill-joy mind, which disgusts us with them as well as with itself. It treats both itself and all that it takes in, whether future or past, according to its insatiable, erratic, and versatile nature.

Unless the vessel's pure, all you pour in turns sour.

—HORACE

~~~~~~~~~~~~~~~~~~~~~~~

The Useful and Polite Art of Carving in 1896

<div align="center">by MARGARET HUNTINGTON HOOKER</div>

I am sure that Poets as well as Cooks are for having Words nicely chosen, and must regret to hear some Persons of Quality say, "Pray cut up that Goose, Help me to some of that Chicken, Hen, or Capon," or "Halve that Plover," not considering how indiscreetly they talk before Men of Art, whose proper Terms are, "Break that Goose, Frust that Chicken, Spoil that Hen, Sauce that Capon, Mince that Plover." If they are so much out in common Things how much more will they be with Herons, Cranes and Peacocks.

To Cut up a Turkey

Raise up the Leg fairly, and open the Joint with the Point of your Knife, but take not off the Leg: then with your Knife lace down both Sides of the Breast and open the Breast-Pinion, but do not take it off: then raise the Merry-Thought betwixt the Breast-Bone and the Top of it: then raise up the Brawn: then turn it Outward upon both Sides, but break it not, nor cut it off: then cut off the Wing-Pinions at the Joint next the Body, and stick each Pinion in the Place you turned the Brawn out: but cut off the sharp End of the Pinion, and take the Middle-Piece, and that will just Fit in its Place. You may Sauce a Capon the same way.

~~~~~~~~~~~~~~~~~~~~~~~

Impressions of a Special Day

by EMILY DICKINSON

From *Bolts of Melody, New Poems of Emily Dickinson*
Copyright, 1945 by the Trustees of Amherst College
Published by Harper & Row, Publishers

I thought the train would never come.
How slow the whistle sang!
I don't believe a peevish bird-
So whimpered for the spring.

I taught my heart a hundred times
Precisely what to say—
Provoking lover, when you came
Its treatise flew away!

To hide my strategy, too late,
To wiser grow, too soon,
For miseries so halcyon
The happiness atone.

* * *

Again his voice is at the door,
I feel the old degree,
I hear him ask the servant
For such an one as me;

I take a flower as I go
My face to justify,
He never saw me in this life,
I might surprise his eye.

I cross the hall with mingled steps,
I silent pass the door,
I look on all this world contains—
Just his face—nothing more!

We talk in venture and in toss,
A kind of plummet strain,
Each sounding shyly just how deep
The other's foot had been.

We walk. I leave my dog behind.
A tender thoughtful moon
Goes with us just a little way
And then we are alone.

Alone—if angels are alone
First time they try the sky!
Alone—if those veiled faces be
We cannot count on high!

I'd give to live that hour again
The purple in my vein;
But he must count the drops himself—
My price for every stain!

The 1840 Style of Mrs. America

From *The Fabulous Forties, 1840–1850* by MEADE MINNIGERODE
Copyright, 1924, by Meade Minnigerode
Published by G. P. Putnam's Sons

In her home, a lady equally capable of entertaining in the parlor and managing in the kitchen found plenty to occupy her in the preparation of her two o'clock dinners—or her formal five o'clock functions at which she ladled out the soup in person at the table, and saw to the placing of the inevitable glass dish of cranberries as carefully as she studied that of her guests—and her eleven o'clock party suppers with their indispensable bowls of hot stewed oysters.

She took pride in her home-made biscuits and cakes—her philpies, bops and zephyrinas, her bachelor's pone, sally lunn and economy cakes, her marvelles, cymbals, jumbles, and journey, or johnny cakes and all the other fifty odd varieties of cake listed in the cook book; she spent hours at her pickling and preserving, and in the manufacture of pastries and pies, custards, puddings, jellies, and essences; she gave the final, personal touches to her trifles and flummeries, her blanc manges, whip syllabubs and floating islands. . . .

And when there was a wedding she took twenty pounds of butter, twenty pounds of sugar, forty pounds of raisins, eighty pounds of currants, twelve pounds of citrons, twenty pounds of flour, twenty nutmegs, twenty glasses of wine, twenty glasses of brandy, two hundred eggs, some cinnamon, mace and cloves, and made a wedding cake.

On her honeymoon she probably went to the Cataract House at Niagara. In which case, in 1841, she was told that: "this is the season when citizens and strangers, and young married folks, are getting ready to visit the great Falls of Niagara. Most of the pleasure of this delightful jaunt is lost by not knowing how to select the route so as to secure despatch, comfort and variety of prospect.

"Proceed direct, after you arrive at Albany, to Syracuse by railroad. This will occupy but eight hours. At Syracuse take the packet boats—by way of relief from car travel—from Syracuse to Oswego; the most beautiful scenery will reward your selection, and in five hours you are at Oswego. Here

· 104 ·

embark on board of one of the splendid steam boats, *United States* or *Saint Lawrence*—floating palaces. After a plentiful repast and a sound sleep, at seven in the morning you will find yourself, refreshed, at Lewiston on the Niagara River, where there is a railroad and commodious cars waiting to convey you to Niagara Falls to breakfast. Thus, without trouble, delay, or any of the usual perplexities incident to travel, you arrive at the Falls in twenty-four hours after you leave Albany —and, what is more important, without the least fatigue."

Thomas Jefferson's Recommendations on Ladies' Dress
From a letter to his daughter

I omitted in that letter to advise you on the subject of dress, which I know you are a little apt to neglect. I do not wish you to be gaily clothed at this time of life, but that your wear should be fine of its kind. But above all things and at all times let your clothes be neat, whole, and properly put on. Do not fancy you must wear them till the dirt is visible to the eye. You will be the last one who is sensible to this. Some ladies think they may, under the privileges of the *déshabillé*, be loose and negligent of their dress in the morning. But be you, from the moment you rise till you go to bed, as cleanly and properly dressed as at the hours of dinner or tea. . . . Nothing is so disgusting to our sex as a want of cleanliness and delicacy in yours. I hope, therefore, the moment you rise from bed, your first work will be to dress yourself in such style, as that you may be seen by any gentleman without his being able to discover a pin amiss, or any other circumstance of neatness wanting.

When Love Can Be Blind

From *The Romance of Greeting Cards* by ERNEST DUDLEY CHASE
Copyright, 1927, by Ernest Dudley Chase

ADVERTISEMENT

Wanted, a wife of amazing perfection,
Of astonishing wit and docile affection,
Of original mind and of great cultivation,
With a proper respect for the lords of creation.

She must have a sweet temper, for mine is not even,
Her eyes must be blue as the azure of heaven,
With rose-tinted cheeks and a smile full of sweetness,
And in dress she must pay great attention to neatness.

She must understand cooking in various branches
From *à la mode* beef down to venison haunches,
Must be swift with her needle, a skillful musician,
An artist, a linguist, a mathematician.

I'm crooked and grouty, I'm old and I'm ugly,
My name's not romantic, Melchisedec Pugly,
But I'm worth half a million; with such an attraction
I yet may set girls at the verge of distraction.

Love's Nearness

by Henry van Dyke

From Goethe's *Nähe des Geliebten*

I think of thee, when golden sunbeams shimmer
      Across the sea;
And when the waves reflect the moon's pale glimmer,
      I think of thee.

I see thy form, when down the distant highway
      The dust-clouds rise;
In deepest night, above the mountain by-way,
      I see thine eyes.

I hear thee when the ocean-tides returning
      Loudly rejoice;
And on the lonely moor, in stillness yearning,
      I hear thy voice.

I dwell with thee: though thou art far removed,
      Yet art thou near.
The sun goes down, the stars shine out,—
      Beloved,
      Ah, wert thou here!

Dean Swift's Recipe for Roast Mutton

Gently Stir and blow the Fire
Lay the Mutton down to roast.
Dress it quickly, I desire,
In the Dripping put a Toast,
That I hunger may remove.
Mutton is the Meat I love.

In the Dresser see it lie;
Oh! the charming White and Red;
Finer Meat ne'er met the eye,
On the sweetest grass it fed:
Let the Jack go swiftly round.
Let me have it nicely browned.

On the Table spread the Cloth
Let the Knives be sharp and clean.
Pickles get and Salad both,
Let them each be fresh and green.
With small Beer, good Ale, and Wine
Oh ye Gods! How I shall dine!

Concerning Friendship

by MARCUS TULLIUS CICERO

In the first place—to whom can life be "worth living," as Ennius says, who does not repose on the mutual kind feeling of some friend? What can be more delightful than to have one to whom you can speak on all subjects just as to yourself? Where would be the great enjoyment in prosperity if you had not one to rejoice in it equally with yourself? And adversity would indeed be difficult to endure without some one who would bear it even with greater regret than yourself.

In short, all other objects that are sought after are severally suited to some one single purpose; riches, that you may spend them; power, that you may be courted; honors, that you may be extolled; pleasures, that you may enjoy them; good health, that you may be exempt from harm, and perform the functions of the body. Whereas friendship comprises the greatest number of objects possible; wherever you turn yourself, it is at hand; shut out of no place, never out of season, never irksome; and therefore we do not use fire and water, as they say, on more occasions than we do friendship. And I am not now speaking of common-place or ordinary friendship (though even that brings delight and benefit), but of real and true friendship, such as belonged to those of whom very few are recorded; for prosperity friendship renders more brilliant, and adversity more supportable, by dividing and communicating it.

And while friendship embraces very many and great advantages, she undoubtedly surpasses all in this, that she shines with a brilliant hope over the future, and never suffers the spirit to be weakened or to sink. Besides, he who looks on a true friend looks, as it were, upon a kind of image of himself; wherefore friends, though absent, are still present; though in poverty, they are rich; though weak, yet in the enjoyment of health; and, what is still more difficult to assert, though dead, they are alive; so entirely does the honor, the memory, the regret of friends attend them; from which circumstance the death of the one seems to be happy, and the life of the other praiseworthy; nay, should you remove from nature the cement of kind feelings, neither a house nor a city will be able to stand; even the cultivation of the land will not continue.

Nay, they tell us that some are accustomed to declare, still more unfeelingly, that friendships should be cultivated for the purpose of protection and assistance, and not for kind feeling or affection; and therefore the less a man possesses of independence and of strength, in the same degree he most earnestly desires friendships; that thence it arises that women seek the support of friendship more than men, and the poor more than the rich, and persons in distress rather than those who are considered prosperous.

If it be not clearly perceived how great is the power of friendship and concord, it can be distinctly inferred from quarrels and dissensions; for what house is there so established, or what state so firmly settled, that may not utterly be overthrown by hatred and dissension?

* * *

Let this, therefore, be established as a primary law concerning friendship, that we expect from our friends only what is honorable, and for our friends' sake do what is honorable; that we should not wait till we are asked; that zeal be ever ready, and reluctance far from us; but that we take pleasure in freely giving our advice; that in our friendship the influence of our friends, when they give good advice, should have great weight; and that this be employed to admonish not only candidly, but even severely, if the case shall require, and that we give heed to it when so employed; for, as to certain persons, whom I understand to have been esteemed wise men in Greece, I am of opinion that some strange notions were entertained by them; but there is nothing which they do not follow up with too great subtlety; among the rest, that excessive friendships should be avoided, lest it should be necessary for one to feel anxiety for many; that every one has enough, and more than enough, of his own affairs; that to be needlessly implicated in those of other people is vexatious; that it was most convenient to hold the reins of friendship as loose as possible, so as either to tighten or slacken them when you please: for they argue that the main point toward a happy life is freedom from care, which the mind can not enjoy if one man be, as it were, in travail for others.

Qualities of a Friend

by WILLIAM PENN

A true Friend unbosoms *freely*, advises *justly*, assists *readily*, adventures *boldly*, takes all *patiently*, defends *courageously*, and continues a Friend *unchangeably*.

These being the Qualities of a Friend, we are to find them before we choose one.

The *Covetous*, the *Angry*, the *Proud*, the *Jealous*, the *Talkative*, cannot but make ill Friends, as well as the *False*.

In short, choose a Friend as thou dost a Wife, *till Death separate you.*

Yet be not a Friend beyond the *Altar*: but let *Virtue* bound thy Friendship: else it is not Friendship, but an Evil Confederacy.

If my *Brother* or *Kinsman* will be my Friend, I ought to prefer him before a Stranger, or I show little Duty or *Nature* to my *Parents*.

And as we ought to prefer our *Kindred* in Point of Affection, so too in Point of *Charity*, if *equally* needing and deserving.

All Things Can Be Borne

by ELIZABETH AKERS

Behold, we live through all things, famine, thirst,
    Bereavement, pain: all grief and misery,
All woe and sorrow; life inflicts its worst
    On soul and body,— but we cannot die
Though we be sick, and tired, and faint, and worn,
Lo, all things can be borne.

*   *   *

Still shall the soul around it call
    The shadows which it gathered here,
And, painted on the eternal wall,
    The Past shall re-appear.

—JOHN GREENLEAF WHITTIER

Only God Has the Key

From *Appreciations of Poetry* by LAFCADIO HEARN

Prologue to the Second Series of *"The Dramatic Idyls"*
by ROBERT BROWNING

"You are sick, that's sure,"—they say:
"Sick of what?"—they disagree.
" 'Tis the brain,"—thinks Doctor A;
" 'Tis the heart,"—holds Doctor B.
"The liver—my life I'd lay!"
"The lungs!" "The lights!" Ah me!
So ignorant of man's whole
Of bodily organs plain to see—
So sage and certain, frank and free,
About what's under lock and key—
Man's soul!

That is to say, even the wisest doctors cannot agree about the simple fact of a man's sickness, nothwithstanding the fact that they have studied anatomy and physiology and osteology, and have examined every part of the body. Yet, although the wisest men of science are obliged to confess that they cannot tell you everything about the body, which can be seen, even ignorant persons think that they know everything about the soul of a man, which cannot be seen at all, and about the mind of a man, to which only God himself has the key.

* * *

For there was never yet philosopher
That could endure the toothache patiently,
However they have writ the style of gods
And made a push at chance and sufferance.

From *Much Ado about Nothing*
(V, i) by Shakespeare

Foolish About Windows

by Carl Sandburg

From *Good Morning, America*, copyright 1928, 1956 by Carl Sandburg
Published by Harcourt, Brace & World, Inc.

I was foolish about windows.
The house was an old one and the windows were small.
I asked a carpenter to come and open the walls and put in
    bigger windows.
"The bigger the window the more it costs," he said.
"The bigger the cheaper," I said.
So he tore off siding and plaster and laths
And put in a big window and bigger windows.
I was hungry for windows.

One neighbor said, "If you keep on you'll be able to see
    everything there is."
I answered, "That'll be all right, that'll be classy enough
    for me."
Another neighbor said, "Pretty soon your house will be all
    windows."
And I said, "Who would the joke be on then?"
And still another. "Those who live in glass houses gather
    no moss."
And I said, "Birds of a feather should not throw stones and
    a soft answer turneth away rats."

Afternoon on a Hill

by EDNA ST. VINCENT MILLAY

I will be the gladdest thing
  Under the sun!
I will touch a hundred flowers
  And not pick one.

I will look at cliffs and clouds
  With quiet eyes,
Watch the wind bow down the grass,
  And the grass rise.

And when lights begin to show
  Up from the town,
I will mark which must be mine,
  And then start down!

Bright Memories, Retain — Dark Memories, Discard

by IDA SCOTT TAYLOR

A day of memories! Take out the old musty life-book, con it over and over again. Never mind the interlineations; they are often the most precious part. Never mind the erasures; don't seek to decipher them; you would better not try to recall them; make the line over them a little heavier, blot them out, pass them over. Doubtless they are things you ought to forget, and if there is anything unpleasant suggested by that old book pass that over too. Happy memories elevate and gladden, unhappy memories depress and sadden us. We have no use for anything that hurts our influence in this world, or makes us a stumbling-block to our neighbor. Therefore, cling to all the sweetness and beauty, the brightness and goodness of the past, but turn down, cross out, and tear away the leaves that carry messages of gloom into your life. Remember that "a merry heart doeth good like a medicine."

The Milkmaid's Song

by CHRISTOPHER MARLOWE

Come, live with me, and be my love,
And we will all the pleasure prove
That valleys, groves, or hills, or field,
Or woods and steepy mountains yield,

Where we will sit upon the rocks,
And see the shepherds feed our flocks,
By shallow rivers, to whose falls
Melodious birds sing madrigals.

And I will make thee beds of roses,
And then a thousand fragrant posies;
A cap of flowers, and a kirtle
Embroidered all with leaves of myrtle,

A gown made of the finest wool,
Which from our pretty lambs we pull;
Slippers lined choicely for the cold,
With buckles of the purest gold;

A belt of straw, and ivy-buds,
With coral clasps and amber studs;
And if these pleasures may thee move,
Come, live with me, and be my love.

Thy silver dishes for thy meat,
As precious as the Gods do eat,
Shall on an ivory table be
Prepared each day for thee and me.

The shepherd swains shall dance and sing
For thy delight each May morning:
If these delights thy mind may move,
Then live with me, and be my love.

To Live with Thee
and Be Thy Love
by Sir Walter Raleigh

If all the world and love were young,
And truth in every shepherd's tongue,
These pretty pleasures might me move
To live with thee, and be thy love.

But time drives flocks from field to fold:
When rivers rage, and rocks grow cold,
Then Philomel becometh dumb,
And age complains of cares to come.

The flowers do fade, and wanton fields
To wayward Winter reckoning yields:
A honey tongue, a heart of gall,
Is fancy's spring, but sorrow's fall.

Thy gowns, thy shoes, thy beds of roses,
Thy cap, thy kirtle, and thy posies,
Soon break, soon wither, soon forgotten;
In folly ripe, in reason rotten.

Thy belt of straw, and ivy-buds,
Thy coral clasps and amber studs,
All these in me no means can move
To come to thee, and be thy love.

What should we talk of dainties then,
Of better meat than's fit for men?
These are but vain: that's only good
Which God hath blest, and sent for food.

But could youth last, and love still breed,
Had joys no date, nor age no need,—
Then those delights my mind might move,
To live with thee, and be thy love.

An Answer

by Ella Wheeler Wilcox

If all the year was summertime,
And all the aim of life
Was just to lilt on like a rhyme—
Then I would be your wife.

If all the days were August days,
And crowned with golden weather,
How happy then through green-clad ways
We two could stray together!

If all the nights were moonlit nights,
And we had naught to do
But just to sit and plan delights,
Then I would wed with you.

If life was all a summer fete,
Its soberest pace the "glide,"
Then I would choose you for my mate,
And keep you at my side.

But winter makes full half the year,
And labor half of life,
And all the laughter and good cheer
Give place to wearing strife.
Days will grow cold, and moons wax old,
And then a heart that's true
Is better far than grace or gold—
And so my love, adieu!
I cannot wed with you.

On the Nature of Folly

From *The Florentine Fior di Virtu of 1491*

Translated by Nicholas Fersin
Library of Congress catalogue card number 53-60047

Folly is the vice contrary to the virtue of prudence, or providence. Plato says that folly may be of many kinds. First of all there are constant madmen, like those who are obviously insane. Others are insane at certain times, at which times they are just like those who are obviously insane, while at other times they are in possession of good reason. Such people are called lunatics. And others are melancholically insane, having been deprived of their mind. These can be of a thousand different types. And then there are the madmen who have little intelligence. These are of four kinds. The first act without thinking, just as the impulse comes, without reasoning. Others do not provide themselves with what they need and do not think of consequences. The third category is in too much of a hurry and does not tolerate any advice in what it does. And finally there are those who out of negligence and laziness do not start, try nor carry out any of the things man should do.

Example

Folly may be compared to the wild bull who by his nature hates anything red. Therefore the hunters who want to kill him dress in red and go where the wild bull is known to be. And immediately, without thinking and without looking around, but only because of his strong impulse, the bull runs after them furiously. The hunters flee & hide behind a tree. The bull, in an effort to strike the hunters, strikes the tree with such fury that he sticks his horns in that tree in such a manner that he cannot pull them out anymore. Then the hunters come out and kill him. And Solomon says: "Never speak to a madman because your words will not please him unless you tell him things which correspond to his will."

And he also says: "Speaking of knowledge or science to a madman is just like speaking to a man who is asleep." And again: "On the path of his folly the madman thinks that every man is insane like him." And he also says: "A madman may be recognized by his laughter. When he laughs he raises his voice and opens his mouth as much as he can. But the wise man laughs with moderation." And he also says: "A violent madman is more dangerous than the mother bear after you take away her cubs." And he says: "Correct the wise man and he will love you, correct the madman and he will hate you." And the proverb says: "Punish a good man and he becomes better, but punish a bad man or a madman and he becomes worse."

Example

Of the vice of folly we read in the Roman Histories. Once upon a time Aristotle and Alexander rode through Macedon preceded by the Emperor's servants on foot who shouted: "Give way to the king Alexander." A madman, seated on a rock in the middle of the road, refused to move. One of the servants tried to push him off, but Aristotle said: "Do not remove one rock from another." He said this, because in fact a madman is not a man.

Reparation

by WILLIAM PENN

If thou hast done an Injury to another, rather own it than defend it. One way thou gainest Forgiveness, the other, thou *doubl'st* the Wrong and Reckoning.

Some oppose Honor to *Submission*: But it can be no Honor to maintain, what it is dishonorable to do.

To confess a Fault, that is none, out of Fear, is indeed *mean*: but not to be afraid of standing in one, is *Brutish*.

We should make more *Haste* to Right our Neighbor, than we do to wrong him, and instead of being Vindictive, we should leave him to be *Judge* of his own Satisfaction.

True Honor will pay *treble* Damages, rather than justify *one* Wrong by *another*.

In such Controversies, it is but too common for some to say, *Both are to blame*, to *excuse* their own *Unconcernedness*, which is a *base Neutrality*. Others will cry, *They are both alike*; thereby involving the Injured with the Guilty, to *mince* the Matter for the Faulty, or cover their own Injustice to the wronged Party.

Fear and *Gain* are great Perverters of Mankind, and where either prevails, the *Judgment* is violated.

The Way That Lovers Use

by Rupert Brooke

From *The Collected Poems of Rupert Brooke*
Copyright, 1915, by Dodd, Mead & Company
Copyright, 1943, by Edward Marsh

THE way that lovers use is this;
    They bow, catch hands, with never a word,
And their lips meet, and they do kiss,
    —So I have heard.

They queerly find some healing so,
    And strange attainment in the touch;
There is a secret lovers know,
    —I have read as much.

And theirs no longer joy nor smart,
    Changing or ending, night or day;
But mouth to mouth, and heart to heart,
    —So lovers say.

Song

by RUPERT BROOKE

"OH! Love," they said, "is King of Kings,
  And Triumph is his crown.
Earth fades in flame before his wings,
  And Sun and Moon bow down."—
But that, I knew, would never do;
  And Heaven is all too high.
So whenever I meet a Queen, I said,
  I will not catch her eye.

"Oh! Love," they said, and "Love," they said,
  "The gift of Love is this;
A crown of thorns about thy head,
  And vinegar to thy kiss!"
But Tragedy is not for me;
  And I'm content to be gay.
So whenever I spied a Tragic Lady,
  I went another way.

And so I never feared to see
  You wander down the street,
Or come across the fields to me
  On ordinary feet.
For what they'd never told me of,
  And what I never knew;
It was that all the time, my love,
  Love would be merely you.

A Christmas Wish

by EUGENE FIELD

I 'd like a stocking made for a giant,
   And a meeting house full of toys,
Then I'd go out in a happy hunt
   For the poor little girls and boys;
Up the street and down the street,
   And across and over the town,
I'd search and find them every one,
   Before the sun went down.

One would want a new jack-knife
   Sharp enough to cut;
One would long for a doll with hair,
   And eyes that open and shut;
One would ask for a china set
   With dishes all to her mind;
One would wish a Noah's ark
   With beasts of every kind.

Some would like a doll's cook-stove
   And a little toy wash tub;
Some would prefer a little drum,
   For a noisy rub-a-dub-dub;
Some would wish for a story book,
   And some for a set of blocks;
Some would be wild with happiness
   Over a new tool-box.

And some would rather have little shoes,
   And other things warm to wear;
For many children are very poor
   And the winter is hard to bear;
I'd buy soft flannels for little frocks,
   And a thousand stockings or so,
And the jolliest little coats and cloaks
   To keep out the frost and snow.

I'd load a wagon with caramels
  And candy of every kind,
And buy all the almond and pecan nuts
  And taffy that I could find;
And barrels and barrels of oranges
  I'd scatter right in the way,
So the children would find them the very first thing
  When they wake on Christmas day.

Our Kind of a Man

by JAMES WHITCOMB RILEY

I

The kind of a man for you and me!
He faces the world unflinchingly,
And smites, as long as the wrong resists,
With a knuckled faith and force like fists:
He lives the life he is preaching of,
And loves where most is the need of love;
His voice is clear to the deaf man's ears,
And his face sublime through the blind man's tears;
The light shines out where the clouds were dim,
And the widow's prayer goes up for him;
The latch is clicked at the hovel door,
And the sick man sees the sun once more,
And out o'er the barren fields he sees
Springing blossoms and waving trees,
Feeling, as only the dying may,
That God's own servant has come that way,
Smoothing the path as it still winds on
Through the golden gate where his loved have gone.

II

The kind of a man for me and you!
However little of worth we do
He credits full, and abides in trust
That time will teach us how more is just.
He walks abroad, and he meets all kinds
Of querulous and uneasy minds,
And, sympathizing, he shares the pain
Of the doubts that rack us, heart and brain;
And, knowing this, as we grasp his hand,
We are surely coming to understand!
He looks on sin with pitying eyes—
E'en as the Lord, since Paradise,—
Else, should we read, Though our sins should glow
As scarlet, they shall be white as snow?—
And feeling still, with a grief half glad,
That the bad are as good as the good are bad,
He strikes straight out for the Right—and he
Is the kind of a man for you and me!

Bits

of

Fun

A Rare Horoscope for the Followers of the Stars

by MIKE ROYKO

From his column in the *Chicago Daily News*

Prof. U.R. Doompt, the noted astrologist, has prepared another in his series of horoscopes, which appear exclusively in this column.

Prof. Doompt's horoscopes, unlike others, are not published regularly because he is unable to devote all of his time to studying the stars.

"Gives me a stiff neck," he has often said. "Besides, you seen one, you seen 'em all."

Many famous persons and institutions consult Prof. Doompt's charts before making any important decisions.

His followers include the fireproofers at McCormick Place; the Chicago weather forecasters; Judge Louis Kizas; the New York Mets; Republican John Waner, and various Arab leaders.

Today Under Your Sign

GENERAL CONDITIONS: You will have a stroke of financial luck and will make a great deal of money. You will lose it immediately.

ARIES, (March 21 to April 19): It might be a good time to visit your dentist for a checkup because somebody has put an electronic listening device in your tooth. Avoid foods cooked by strangers.

TAURUS, (April 20 to May 20): Things will get much worse before they get better. Then they will get even worse. Stars indicate that your secretary is cheating on you.

GEMINI, (May 20 to June 21): Conditions are excellent for making application for membership in the Blackstone Rangers or the Black Muslims. If they turn you down for reasons of race or religion, file a complaint with the Chicago Commission on Human Relations.

CANCER, (June 22 to July 21): A good day for starting a new life for yourself. Run away, change your name, grow long sideburns and a bushy moustache. Don't worry, your husband will get over it.

LEO, (July 22 to Aug. 21): If you are out for the evening, rush home immediately. Your baby-sitter and some friends are drinking up all of your liquor. So are your children.

VIRGO, (Aug. 22 to Sept. 22): Do not get excited, but a tall, swarthy, mysterious stranger wearing a derby hat is crouching in a tree in your yard. Conditions are excellent for changing socks.

LIBRA, (Sept. 23 to Oct. 22): Begin making plans for the future, as your employer is planning to replace you with a machine. Your TV set is watching you.

SCORPIO, (Oct. 23 to Nov. 21): Do not wear a miniskirt to the office today. And do not let your wife wear one, either. Count your toes sometime this afternoon. You might be surprised at the results.

SAGITTARIUS, (Nov. 22 to Dec. 21): Look inside your refrigerator. A tiny thief may be hiding there. Conditions are excellent for taking a home study course in tap-dancing; your grandchildren will be impressed.

CAPRICORN, (Dec. 22 to Jan. 20): While you were working your wife withdrew your savings, sold the car, bought a motorcycle and ran off with a folk singer. Good day to have your dog checked for worms or to putter about in the yard.

AQUARIUS, (Jan. 21 to Feb. 19): Your scale is wrong. You weigh 15 pounds more than it shows. Before you put your shoes on, look inside them. One never knows.

PISCES, (Feb. 20 to March 20): Things seen under this sign are too terrible to mention. Don't move. Stay right there until help arrives, if it does.

A Good Watch
Is a Good Watch
Until the Repairers Get at It

by MARK TWAIN

My beautiful new watch had run eighteen months without losing or gaining, and without breaking any part of its machinery or stopping. I had come to believe it infallible in its judgments about the time of day, and to consider its constitution

and its anatomy imperishable. But at last, one night, I let it run down. I grieved about it as if it were a recognized messenger and forerunner of calamity. But by-and-by I cheered up, set the watch by guess, and commanded my bodings and superstitions to depart. Next day I stepped into the chief jeweller's to set it by the exact time, and the head of the establishment took it out of my hand and proceeded to set it for me. Then he said, "She is four minutes slow—regulator wants pushing up." I tried to stop him—tried to make him understand that the watch kept perfect time. But no; all this human cabbage could see was that the watch was four minutes slow, and the regulator *must* be pushed up a little; and so, while I danced around him in anguish, and beseeched him to let the watch alone, he calmly and cruelly did the shameful deed.

My watch began to gain. It gained faster and faster day by day. Within the week it sickened to a raging fever, and its pulse went up to 150 in the shade. At the end of two months it had left all the timepieces of the town far in the rear, and was a fraction over thirteen days ahead of the almanac. It was away into November enjoying the snow, while the October leaves were still turning. It hurried up house-rent, bills payable, and such things, in such a ruinous way that I could not abide it.

I took it to the watchmaker to be regulated. He asked me if I had ever had it repaired. I said no, it had never needed any repairing. He looked a look of vicious happiness and eagerly pried the watch open, then put a small dice-box into his eye and peered into its machinery. He said it wanted cleaning and oiling, besides regulating—come in a week.

After being cleaned and oiled and regulated, my watch slowed down to that degree that it ticked like a tolling bell. I began to be left by trains, I failed all appointments, I got to missing my dinner; my watch strung out three days' grace to four, and let me go to protest; I gradually drifted back into yesterday, then day before, then into last week, and by-and-by the comprehension came upon me that all solitary and alone I was lingering along in week before last, and the world was out of sight. I seemed to detect in myself a sort of sneaking fellow-feeling for the mummy in the museum, and a desire to swap news with him.

I went to a watchmaker again. He took the watch all to pieces while I waited, and then said the barrel was "swelled." He said he could reduce it in three days. After this the watch *averaged* well, but nothing more. For half a day it would go like the very mischief, and keep up such a barking and wheezing, and whooping and sneezing and snorting, that I could not hear myself think for the disturbance; and as long as it held out there was not a watch in the land that stood any chance against it. But the rest of the day it would keep on slowing down and fooling along until all the clocks it had left behind caught up again. So at last, at the end of twenty-four hours, it would trot up to the judges' stand all right and just in time. It would show a fair and square average, and no man could say it had done more or less than its duty. But a correct average is only a mild virtue in a watch, and I took this instrument to another watchmaker. He said the kingbolt was broken. I said I was glad it was nothing more serious. To tell the plain truth, I had no idea what the kingbolt was, but I did not choose to appear ignorant to a stranger. He repaired the kingbolt, but what the watch gained in one way it lost in another. It would run a while and then stop a while, and then run a while again, and so on, using its own discretion about the intervals. And every time it went off it kicked back like a musket.

I padded my breast for a few days, but finally took the watch to another watchmaker. He picked it all to pieces and turned the ruin over and over under his glass; and then he said there appeared to be something the matter with the hair-trigger. He fixed it, and gave it a fresh start. It did well now, except that always at ten minutes to ten the hands would shut together like a pair of scissors, and from that time forth they would travel together.

The oldest man in the world could not make head or tail of the time of day by such a watch, and so I went again to have the thing repaired. This person said that the crystal had got bent, and that the mainspring was not straight. He also

remarked that part of the works needed half-soling. He made these things all right, and then my timepiece performed un-exceptionably, save that now and then, after working along quietly for nearly eight hours, everything inside would let go all of a sudden and begin to buzz like a bee, and the hands would straightway begin to spin round and round so fast that their individuality was lost completely, and they simply seemed a delicate spider's web over the face of the watch. She would reel off the next twenty-four hours in six or seven minutes, and then stop with a bang.

I went with a heavy heart to one more watchmaker, and looked on while he took her to pieces. Then I prepared to cross-question him rigidly, for this thing was getting serious. The watch had cost two hundred dollars originally, and I seemed to have paid out two or three thousand for repairs.

While I waited and looked on I presently recognized in this watchmaker an old acquaintance — a steamboat engineer of other days, and not a good engineer either. He examined all the parts carefully, just as the other watchmakers had done, and then delivered his verdict with the same confidence of manner. He said—

"She makes too much steam—you want to hang the monkey-wrench on the safety-valve!"

I brained him on the spot, and had him buried at my own expense.

My uncle William (now deceased alas!) used to say that a good horse was a good horse until it had run away once, and that a good watch was a good watch until the repairers got a chance at it. And he used to wonder what became of all the unsuccessful tinkers, and gun-smiths, and shoe-makers, and blacksmiths; but nobody could ever tell him.

A Diary Can Be Troublesome

From *The Cynic's Word Book* by AMBROSE BIERCE
Copyright, 1906, by Doubleday, Page & Company

Sam kept a diary wherein were writ
So many noble deeds and so much wit
That the Recording Angel, when Sam died,
Erased all entries of his own and cried:
"I'll judge you by your diary." Said Sam:
"Thank you; 't will show you what a saint I am"—
Straightway producing, jubilant and proud,
That record from a pocket in his shroud.
The Angel slowly turned the pages o'er,
Each lying line of which he knew before,
Glooming and gleaming as by turns he hit
On noble action and amusing wit;
Then gravely closed the book and gave it back.
"My friend, you've wandered from your proper track;
You'd never be content this side the tomb—
For deeds of greatness Heaven has little room,
And Hell's no latitude for making mirth,"
He said, and kicked the fellow back to earth.

A Swarm of Bees

B patient, B prayerful, B humble, B mild,
B wise as a Solon, B meek as a child;
B studious, B thoughtful, B loving, B kind,
B sure you make matter subservient to mind.
B cautious, B prudent, B trustful, B true,
B courteous to all men, B friendly with few.
B temperate in argument, pleasure, and wine,
B careful of conduct, of money, of time.
B cheerful, B grateful, B hopeful, B firm,
B peaceful, benevolent, willing to learn;
B courageous, B gentle, B liberal, B just,
B aspiring, B humble, BECAUSE thou art dust;
B penitent, circumspect, sound in the faith,
B active, devoted, B faithful till death;
B honest, B holy, transparent, and pure,
B dependent, B Christlike, and you'll B secure.

From Miss Bea Mine
222 maiden Lane
Heartsville, Ill.

To Miss Bea M
222 maid
Heartsvill

A Mail Order Marriage Mill and Other Schemes

In about the year 1880, a man in East Orange, New Jersey, solicited business by means of the following remarkable circular:

Would you like to get married?

If so, we will give you the names of twenty persons, either male or female, who would like to have the pleasure of writing to you or seeing you. We have both classes, the rich as well as the poor.

If you do not care to marry, and would like to have some fun, send to us for the fun list; life is too short to be wasted away doing nothing and knowing nothing, so have a little fun while it is going. Which list will you have, our marriage list or our fun list?

To get the list you must send us 10 cents and the names of five single persons.

Remember, girls, this is leap year. Boys, look out, or they will be after you.

Send 50 cents and join our Fun and Frolic Club for one year.

If you are already married, please hand this circular to some friend who is not.

Those who desired the "marriage list" were required to send twenty cents and five new names, and a list of twenty men or women who desired to correspond with a view to matrimony was sent in return. A young Jerseyman who sent for the "fun and frolic list" received a list of twenty women and twenty men, residing at various points in Pennsylvania and the Western states. It was thought at first that the swindler was amenable to the postal laws, but there was no perceptible fraud, and hence nothing could be done.

* * *

Every Generation Has Been Plagued by Taxes

*A recital of English taxes of the mid-1800's —
all too familiar today*

Taxes upon every article which enters the mouth, or covers the back, or is placed under the foot; taxes upon everything which is pleasant to see, hear, feel, smell, and taste; taxes upon warmth, light, and locomotion; taxes on everything on earth, and the waters under the earth; on everything that comes from abroad, or is grown at home; taxes on the raw material; taxes on every fresh value that is added to it by the industry of man; taxes on the sauce which pampers man's appetite, and the drug that restores him to health; on the ermine which decorates the judge, and the rope which hangs the criminal; on the poor man's salt, and the rich man's spice; on the brass nails of the coffin, and the ribbons of the bride; at bed and board, couchant or levant, we must pay.

The schoolboy whips his taxed top; the beardless youth manages his taxed horse with a taxed bridle on a taxed road; and the dying Englishman, pouring his medicine, which has paid seven per cent, into a spoon which has paid fifteen per cent, flings himself back upon his chintz bed, which has paid twenty-two per cent, makes his will on an eight-pound stamp, and expires in the arms of an apothecary who has paid a licence of a hundred pounds for the privilege of putting him to death. His whole property is then immediately taxed from two to ten per cent. Besides the probate, large fees are demanded for burying him in the chancel; his virtues are handed down to posterity on taxed marble; and he is then gathered to his fathers —to be taxed no more.

The Greedy Tax Collector

by Gassalasca Jape, S.J.

From *The Cynic's Word Book* by Ambrose Bierce
Copyright, 1906, by Doubleday, Page & Company

In ancient times there lived a king
Whose tax-collectors could not wring
From all his subjects gold enough
To make the royal way less rough.
For pleasure's highway, like the dames
Whose premises adjoin it, claims
Perpetual repairing. So
The tax-collectors in a row
Appeared before the throne to pray
Their master to devise some way
To swell the revenue. "So great,"
Said they, "are the demands of state
A tithe of all that we collect
Will scarcely meet them. Pray reflect:
How, if one-tenth we must resign,
Can we exist on t'other nine?"

The monarch asked them in reply:
"Has it occurred to you to try
The advantage of economy?"
"It has," the spokesman said: "we sold
All of our gay garrotes of gold;
With plated-ware we now compress
The necks of those whom we assess.
Plain iron forceps we employ
To mitigate the miser's joy
Who hoards, with greed that never tires,
That which your Majesty requires."
Deep lines of thought were seen to plow
Their way across the royal brow.
"Your state is desperate, no question;
Pray favor me with a suggestion."
"O King of Men," the spokesman said,
"If you'll impose upon each head
A tax, the augmented revenue
We'll cheerfully divide with you."

As flashes of the sun illume
The parted storm-cloud's sullen gloom,
The king smiled grimly. "I decree
That it be so — and, not to be
In generosity outdone,
Declare you, each and every one,
Exempted from the operation
Of this new law of capitation.
But lest the people censure me
Because they're bound and you are free,
'T were well some clever scheme were laid
By you this poll-tax to evade.
I'll leave you now while you confer
With my most trusted minister."
The monarch from the throne-room walked
And straightway in among them stalked
A silent man, with brow concealed,
Bare-armed — his gleaming axe revealed!

Mr. and Mrs. Discobbolos

by EDWARD LEAR

I

Mr. and Mrs. Discobbolos
    Climbed to the top of a wall.
And they sate to watch the sunset sky
And to hear the Nupiter Piffkin cry
    And the Biscuit Buffalo call.
They took up a roll and some Camomile tea,
And both were as happy as happy could be—
        Till Mrs. Discobbolos said,—
        "Oh! W! X! Y! Z!
        "It has just come into my head—
    "Suppose we should happen to fall ! ! ! ! !
            "Darling Mr. Discobbolos!"

II

"Suppose we should fall down flumpetty
    "Just like pieces of stone!
"On to the thorns,—or into the moat!
"What would become of your new green coat?
    "And might you not break a bone?
"It never occurred to me before—
"That perhaps we shall never go down any more!"
        And Mrs. Discobbolos said—
        Oh! W! X! Y! Z!
    "What put it into your head
"To climb up this wall?—my own
                "Darling Mr. Discobbolos!"

III

Mr. Discobbolos answered,—
    "At first it gave me pain,—
"And I felt my ears turn perfectly pink
"When your exclamation made me think
    "We might never get down again!
"But now I believe it is wiser far
"To remain for ever just where we are."—
        And Mr. Discobbolos said,
        "Oh! W! X! Y! Z!
    "It has just come into my head—
"——We shall never go down again—
                "Dearest Mrs. Discobbolos!"

IV

So Mr. and Mrs. Discobbolos
    Stood up, and began to sing,
"Far away from hurry and strife
"Here we will pass the rest of life,
    "Ding a dong, ding dong, ding!
"We want no knives nor forks nor chairs,
"No tables nor carpets nor household cares,
    "From worry of life we've fled—
    "Oh! W! X! Y! Z!
    "There is no more trouble ahead,
"Sorrow or any such thing—
                "For Mr. and Mrs. Discobbolos!"

The New Vestments

by EDWARD LEAR

There lived an old man in the Kingdom of Tess,
Who invented a purely original dress;
And when it was perfectly made and complete,
He opened the door, and walked into the street.

By way of a hat he'd a loaf of Brown Bread,
In the middle of which he inserted his head;—
His Shirt was made up of no end of dead Mice,
The warmth of whose skins was quite fluffy and nice;—
His Drawers were of Rabbit-skins;—so were his Shoes;—
His Stockings were skins,—but it is not known whose;—
His Waistcoat and Trowsers were made of Pork Chops;—
His Buttons were Jujubes, and Chocolate Drops;—
His Coat was all Pancakes with Jam for a border,
And a girdle of Biscuits to keep it in order;
And he wore over all, as a screen from bad weather,
A Cloak of green Cabbage-leaves stitched all together.

He had walked a short way, when he heard a great noise,
Of all sorts of Beasticles, Birdlings, and Boys;—
And from every long street and dark lane in the town
Beasts, Birdles, and Boys in a tumult rushed down.
Two Cows and a Calf ate his Cabbage-leaf Cloak;—
Four Apes seized his Girdle, which vanished like smoke;—
Three Kids ate up half of his Pancaky Coat,—
And the tails were devour'd by an ancient He Goat;—
An army of Dogs in a twinkling tore *up* his
Pork Waistcoat and Trowsers to give to their Puppies;—
And while they were growling, and mumbling the Chops,
Ten Boys prigged the Jujubes and Chocolate Drops.—
He tried to run back to his house, but in vain,
For Scores of fat Pigs came again and again;—
They rushed out of stables and hovels and doors,—
They tore off his stockings, his shoes, and his drawers;—
And now from the housetops with screechings descend,
Striped, spotted, white, black, and gray Cats without end,
They jumped on his shoulders and knocked off his hat,—
When Crows, Ducks, and Hens made a mincemeat of that;—

They speedily flew at his sleeves in a trice,
And utterly tore up his Shirt of dead Mice;—
They swallowed the last of his Shirt with a squall,—
Whereon he ran home with no clothes on at all.

And he said to himself as he bolted the door,
"I will not wear a similar dress any more,
"Any more, any more, any more, never more!"

* * *

O for one hour of youthful joy!
    Give back my twentieth spring!
I'd rather laugh a bright-haired boy
    Than reign a gray-beard king!

OLIVER WENDELL HOLMES

A Loud Cackle for Just an Average Egg

From *The Cynic's Word Book* by AMBROSE BIERCE
Copyright, 1906, by Doubleday, Page & Company

They say that hens do cackle loudest when
 There's nothing vital in the egg they've laid;
 And there are hens, professing to have made
A study of mankind, who say that men
Whose business is to drive the tongue or pen
 Make the most clamorous fanfaronade
 O'er their most worthless work; and I'm afraid
In this respect they're really like the hen.
Lo! the drum-major in his coat of gold,
 His blazing breeches and high-towering cap,
Imperiously pompous, "bloody, bold
 And resolute"—an awe-inspiring chap!
Who'd think this gorgeous hero's only virtue
Is that in battle he will never hurt you?

"I Would That I Were Rich"

A parody of TENNYSON's *Mariana* that applies to all

With black coal-dust the walls and floor
 Were thickly coated one and all;
 On rusty hinges swung the door
 That open'd to the gloomy wall;
 The broken chairs looked dull and dark,
 Undusted was the mantel-piece,

And deeply speck'd with spots of grease
Within, the chamber of the clerk.
  He only said, "I'm very weary
    With living in this ditch;"
  He said, "I am confounded dreary,
    I would that I were rich."

His bills came with the bells at even;
  His bills came ere their sound had died;
He could not think why bills were given,
  Except to torture clerks—and sigh'd.
And when the flickering rushlight's flame
  In darkness deep could scarce be seen,
  He mutter'd forth his bottled spleen,
Unheard by aught of mortal frame.
  He said, "My life is very dreary
    With living in this ditch;"
  He said, "I am tarnation weary,
    I would that I were rich."

Upon the middle of the bed,
  Sleeping, he dream'd of hoarded gold;
Sovereigns were jingling in his head,
  And in his ken was wealth untold.
But when he woke, no hope of change,
  In silver or in circumstance,
  Before his sorrowing eyes did dance;
He thought that it was very strange—
  But only said, "My life is dreary,
    I'll go to sleep," he said;
  He said "I am infernal weary,
    I would that bill were paid."

About six fathoms from the wall,
  A blackened chimney (much askew)
Smoked in his face—and round and small
  The chimney-pots destroy his view,
Hard by—a popular highway,
  With coal-dust turned to pitchy dark,
  Where many a little dog doth bark,
Some black, some mottled, many grey.
  He only said, "My life is dreary
    With living in this ditch;"
  He said, "I am fatigued and weary,
    I would that I were rich."

Jack Gay, Abroad and at Home, or The Party Boy Unmasked

by Laman Blanchard

Conveniences and customs of life may change,
but human nature remains the same.

Who that had once met Jack Gay at dinner, where'er the feast of venison and the flow of port prevailed, ever forgot him! What lady, the luckiest of her sex, ever experienced his "delicate attentions" at a quiet evening party, a quiet concert, or a quiet dance, without speaking of him from that moment, not as the most charming of acquaintances, but as a very old friend—without feeling quite sure that she had known him all her life, though she had never seen him but that once?

What spirits he had! Other men had their jovial moods, but Jack was always jovial. To be lively by fits and starts, to be delightful when the humor sets in, to emulate the fair exquisite of Pope,

"And make a lover happy—*for a whim—*"

is within anybody's reach. But Jack had no fits and starts; the humor flowed in one unebbing course, and his whim consisted in making everybody as happy as he was at all seasons.

His joviality never depended upon the excellence of a dinner, the choice of wines, or any accident of the hour. His high spirits and invariable urbanity were wholly independent of the arrangements of the table, the selection of the guests, and the topics of conversation. He discovered pleasant things to hearken to, and found delightful themes to chat upon, even during the dreary twenty minutes before dinner. Yes, even *that* was a lively time to Jack. Whenever he went out it was to enjoy a pleasant evening, and he enjoyed it.

The fish was spoil'd, the soup was cold,
The meat was broil'd, the jokes were old,
The tarts were dumps, the wine not cool,
The guests were pumps, the host a fool—

but for all this Jack cared about as much as a flying-fish cares for a shower of rain. No combination of ill omens and perverse accidents ever proved a damper to him.

He is invited to meet (say) Johnson and Burke, and is greeted, on his entrance, with the well-known tidings that

Johnson and Burke "couldn't come." Does Jack heave one sigh in compliment to the illustrious absentees, and in depreciation of the company who *have* assembled? Not he. No momentary shade of disappointment dims his smiling face. He seems as delighted to meet the little parlor-full of dull people, as though the room were crammed with Crichtons. He has the honor of being presented to little Miss Somebody, from the country, who seems shy; and he takes the same pains to show his pleasure in the introduction, and to tempt the timid stranger to talk, that he would have exerted in an effort to interest Mrs. Siddons. He sits next to a solemn ignoramus, who is facetious in expounding the humors of Squire Bog, his neighbor, or didactic in developing the character of Dogsby the great patriot in his parish; and Jack listens as complacently as though his ear were being regaled with new-born bons mots of Sheridan's, or anecdotes of the Earl of Chatham.

Jack, like some statesmen, was born to be out; and to him, as to some other statesmen, all parties were the same. The only preference he ever seemed to entertain was for the particular party that chanced at the particular moment to rejoice in his presence. He enjoyed everything that happened. Leigh Hunt, describing a servant-maid "at the play," observes, that every occurrence of the evening adds to her felicity—for she likes even the waiting between the acts, which is tiresome to others. So with Jack at a party. He enjoyed some dislocated experiments on the harp, by an astonishing child, aged only fifteen; and was the sole person in the room who encored with *sincerity* that little prodigy's convulsive edition of "Bid me discourse." He listened with laudable gravity to Master Henry's recitation of "Rolla's Address," and suggested the passages in which John Kemble was rather too closely followed. He enjoyed the glasses of warm wine handed round between the songs; he liked the long flat pauses, "when nobody said nothing to his neighbor;" and he liked the sudden burst of gabble in which, at the termination of the pause, as if by preconcerted agreement, every creature eagerly joined.

He liked the persons he had never met before, and those whom he was in the habit of meeting just seven times a week. He admired the piano that was always out of tune, and the lady who, kindly consenting to play, was always out of temper. He thought the persons to whom he had not been introduced very agreeable, and all the rest extremely entertaining. He was delighted with his evening, whether it exploded in a grand supper, or went-off, flash-in-the-pan fashion, with a sandwich.

He never bottled up his best things, to uncork them in a more brilliant company the next night; he was never dull because he was expected to shine, and never, by laborious efforts to shine, succeeded in showing that dullness was his forte. He pleased everybody because he was pleased himself; and he was himself pleased, because he could not help it. Many queer-looking young men sang better, but nobody sang with such promptness and good taste; many awkward gawkies danced with more exactness and care, but nobody danced so easily to himself or so acceptably to his partner; many handsome dashing fellows were more showy and imposing in their manners, but none produced the agreeable effect that followed a few words of his, or one of his joyous laughs—nay even a kind and sprightly glance. The elaborate and long meditated impromptu of the reputed wit fell still-born, while one of Jack's unstudied gay-hearted sallies burst like a rocket, and showered sparkles over the room.

Everybody went away convinced that there was one human being in the world whose oasis of life had no surrounding desert. Jack lived but for enjoyment. The links of the chain that bound him to existence were of pure gold—there was no rough iron clanking between. He seemed sent into the world to show how many may be amused, cheered, comforted, by one light heart. That heart appeared to tell him, that where his fellow-creatures were, it was impossible to be dull; and the spirit of this assurance prevailed in all he said and did; for if he staid till the last half dozen dropped off, he was just as fresh and jocund as when the evening began. He never knew what it was to be tired, and as the hospitable door was at last closed upon him, you heard him go laughing away down the steps. Upon his tomb indeed might be written a paraphrase of the epitaph so gloriously earned by his illustrious namesake:—

> So that the merry and the wise might say,
> Pressing their jolly bosoms, "Here *laughs* Gay!"

But did anybody, who may happen to see this page, ever see the aforesaid Jack at home?—at high-noon, or in the evening when *preparing to go out!* Behold him on the eve of departure—just going—about to plunge, at the appointed moment, into the revelries of a brilliant circle, where, if he were not, a score of sweet voices would fall to murmuring "I wish he were here!" For the admiration, the envy, the cordial liking

which surely await him there, you would now be apt to substitute commiseration, regret—a bit of friendly advice to him
to stop at home, and a pull at the bell for pen-and-ink that he
might write an excuse.

The truth is, that Jack was a morbid, irresolute, wayward,
cross-grained chap. He was kind-hearted in the main, and even
generous; but his temper was often sullen, and his spirit often
cynical. Catch him on a winter's afternoon, half an hour before
he dressed for dinner! You would think him twenty years older,
and five bottle-noses uglier. You would conclude that he was
going to dine with Diogenes in his tub, or to become a par-
taker of a skeleton-feast in Surgeons'-hall. The last time we
ever saw Jack out of company, he was in such a mood as we
have hinted at. It was a November afternoon between five and
six—there was no light in the room—but by the melancholy
gleam of a low fire, he was to be seen seated on a music-stool
with his feet on the fender, his elbows on his knees, his head
resting upon his hands, and his eyes listlessly wandering over
the dull coals in search of the picturesque.

"Come in!" growled the voice of the Charmer. "Can you
grope your way? Dreary rooms these—and lights make 'em
worse."

Then without moving his seat to give us a share of the fire,
he applied the poker to the cinders, not to kindle a blaze and
throw a light upon the gloom, but evidently to put out any
little stray flame that might happen to be lingering there. There
was just light enough to show that his face wore an air of
profound sadness and despondency. To a serious inquiry as
to the cause—if anything had happened,

"Yes," murmured the Fascinator, with an amiable scowl,
"the weather has happened, November has happened, and
dinner will happen in another hour. Here's a night to go three
miles for a slice of saddle o' mutton! My luck! Cold and wet,
isn't it?" continued the Irresistible, knocking cinder after cinder
into the ashes; "I'm miserable enough at home, and so forsooth,
I must dress and go out. Ugh! This is what they call having
a pleasant life of it. I don't know what you may think, but I
look upon an invitation to dinner as nothing less than an insult.
Why should I be dragged out of my wretched nook here,
without an appetite, and against my will? We call this a free
country, where nobody's allowed to be miserable in his own
way—where every man's a slave to ceremony—a victim to his
own politeness, a martyr to civil notes. Here's my saddle o'

mutton acquaintance, for example; I never hurt or offended the man in all my days, and yet I must go and dine with him. I'd rather go to a funeral. Well, if you've anything to say, out with it—for my hour's come. Now mind, before I ring this bell, I predict that there's no hot water, and that my boots are damp."

The difference between Jack at six, and Jack at seven, was the difference between a clock down and a clock wound up— between a bird in the shell, and a bird on the wing—between a bowl of punch before, and after, the spirit is poured in,— it was the difference between Philip drunk and Philip sober (or the reverse if you will)—between a lord mayor in his plain blue-coat and kerseys, and a lord mayor in his state robes;— between Grimaldi at the side-scene waiting to go on, with that most melancholy shadow on his face which tradition has so touchingly painted, and Grimaldi on the stage, in view of the convulsed spectators, the illuminator of congregated dull-ness, the instantaneous disperser of the blues, the explorer of every crevice of the heart wherein care can lurk—an embodied grin. It was the difference, to speak more exactly still, between Sappho at her toilet, and Sappho at an evening mask.

To see Jack when just beginning to prepare for a drop-in somewhere, late at night—between ten and twelve—was almost as good as seeing him when arrived there. The rash promise made, he always contrived to fulfill it—though it was often ten chances to one that he did not, and he appeared to keep his engagements by miracle. As the hour drew nigh, you would imagine that he had just received tidings of the dreadful loss of several relatives per railroad, or that half his income had been swallowed up in a mine, or forged exchequer-bills. It would be impossible to conjecture that his shrugs and sighs, peevish gestures and muttered execrations, were but the dark shadows of a brilliant "coming event"— that discontent and mortification were the forerunners of the gay Hours, and that bitter moroseness, limping and growling, announced the approach of the dancing Pleasures!

So it was; for Jack at that moment, instead of hailing these dancing Pleasures by anticipation, and meeting them at least half-way, would gladly have ridden ten miles in any other direction. He could make himself tolerably comfortable any-where, save at the place to which he was ruthlessly, imperi-ously bound—with anybody, save with the people who were anxiously waiting for a glimpse of his good-humored visage.

He was fully bent on going, in fact he felt that he must; yet he raised every obstacle that ill-temper could invent, knowing all the while that he should be obliged to surmount them.

He would even allow his reluctance to stir, to prevail so far over the gentlemanly principle of his nature, as to question secretly within himself whether he *ought* to go, while he entertained a suspicion that the people who had again invited him were not *quite* prudent in giving so many expensive parties!

He would catch hold of any rag of an acquaintance just then, to cover his loneliness, and to save him from utter solitude; to give him an excuse for procrastinating, and an opportunity of grumbling out his regrets at stripping from head to foot, not to go to bed, but to go *out;* at being doomed to shake off his quiet moping mood, and plunge head-foremost into festivity. And then, when the effort had been made, when the last obstacle had been overcome, when he was arrayed from top to toe, and could no longer complain of this thing not in readiness, and that thing mislaid, or the glove that split in drawing it on, or the cab that was not (*and never was*) on the stand when he wanted one, he would ask himself with a deep-drawn sigh the melancholy question: "Isn't it hard that a man *must* go out, with a broken heart, to take an hour or two's jollification at this time of night?"

Off went Jack Gay; and until four in the morning the merry Hours lagged far behind his joyous spirits. Hospitality put on his magic boots to run a race with him, and the bewitching eyes of Pleasure herself looked grave and sleepy compared with the glistening orbs of her votary!

Cupid

An Anacreontic fable

Cupid, a spoiled and peevish boy,
Is always wanting some new toy;
And what is more, his mother Venus
Never denies—*quodcunque genus*—
Any odd thing the urchin fancies,
From kings and queens to scullery Nancies.
His fondling mother, t' other day,
Gave him some hearts wherewith to play;
No sooner did the rascal take them,
Than he began to bruise and break them!

GEORGE CRUIKSHANK'S *Omnibus*

Ike Walton's Prayer

by JAMES WHITCOMB RILEY

I crave, dear Lord,
   No boundless hoard
   Of gold and gear,
      Nor jewels fine,
      Nor lands, nor kine,
Nor treasure-heaps of anything.—
      Let but a little hut be mine
   Where at the hearthstone I may hear
         The cricket sing,
         And have the shine
   Of one glad woman's eyes to make,
   For my poor sake,
      Our simple home a place divine;—
Just the wee cot—the cricket's chirr—
Love, and the smiling face of her.

I pray not for
Great riches, nor
   For vast estates, and castle-halls,—
   Give me to hear the bare footfalls
      Of children o'er
      An oaken floor
   New-rinsed with sunshine, or bespread
   With but the tiny coverlet
   And pillow for the baby's head;
And, pray Thou, may
The door stand open and the day
   Send ever in a gentle breeze,
   With fragrance from the locust-trees,
      And drowsy moan of doves, and blur
   Of robin-chirps, and drone of bees,
      With afterhushes of the stir
   Of intermingling sounds, and then
      The good-wife and the smile of her
   Filling the silences again
      The cricket's call,
         And the wee cot,
      Dear Lord of all,
         Deny me not!

I pray not that
Men tremble at
My power of place
And lordly sway,—
I only pray for simple grace
To look my neighbor in the face
Full honestly from day to day—
Yield me his horny palm to hold,
And I'll not pray
For gold;—
The tanned face, garlanded with mirth,
It hath the kingliest smile on earth—
The swart brow, diamonded with sweat,
Hath never need of coronet.
And so I reach,
Dear Lord, to Thee,
And do beseech
Thou givest me
The wee cot, and the cricket's chirr,
Love, and the glad sweet face of her!

When the Streams Rise
A call to all fishermen
by THOMAS TOD STODDART

I

When the streams rise,
When the wind flies,
With hope and delight we grow dizzy,
And all a-near
Airy words hear
Be busy, sweet angler, be busy.

II

Then we prepare
Tackle and hair,
And levy fair minnows full plenty,
Or armed with hoe
A-gathering go
Of brandlings and dew-feeders dainty.

III
Then from the spring
Mosses we bring
To store our fresh baits before starting,
Young and unshorn,
Green in the horn,
Culled when the clouds are departing.

IV
Thus duly stored
Cunning or froward
No fish can say nay to our tackle,
While each we ply,
Worm, pink and fly,
Grey palmer or liveried hackle.

V
Heigh for a wind
Gushing behind!
Heigh for a cloud dark and showery!
Foamy and freed,
Let the stream speed
Under the willow-bough flowery.

VI
So may we start,
Joyous in heart
With hope and felicity dizzy,
And still a-near
Airy words hear
Be busy, sweet angler, be busy!

Josh Billings' Philosophy
An earthy view of people and living

If you want to get at the circumference of a man, examine him among men; but if you want to get at his actual diameter, measure him at his fireside.

There are but few men who have character enough to lead a life of idleness.

A puppy plays with every pup he meets, but old dogs have few associates.

There is no such thing as flattery. If commendation is deserved, it is not flattery but truth; if commendation is not deserved, it is not flattery but slander.

Beauty that doesn't make a woman vain makes her very beautiful.

It costs a good deal to be wise, but it doesn't cost anything to be happy.

True love is spelled just the same in Choctaw as it is in English.

Hope is everybody's handmaid; she is a sly coquette and promises many favors, but grants only a few, and they are badly discounted.

The most bitter sarcasm sleeps in silent words.

I hold that a man has just as much right to spell a word as it is pronounced as he has to pronounce it the way it isn't spelled.

He who buys what he doesn't need will, ere long, need what he can't buy.

There is nothing so difficult to hide as our follies.

"The luxury of grief!" This, I take it, means to have your old uncle die and leave you $9,000, and you cry.

Necessity begot Invention — Invention begot Convenience — Convenience begot Pleasure—Pleasure begot Luxury—Luxury begot Riot and Disease, who between them begot Poverty— and Poverty begot Necessity again. This is the revolution of man.

The Old-Time Circus Clown

by Frank L. Staunton

I wonder where's the circus clown, with all his fun and noise,
The feller who jest ruled the ring, when you and me was boys?
There's lot o' funny fellers now that travel with the show.
But where's the old-time circus clown, we all knowed long ago?

I remember, like 'twas yesterday, his every smile and frown—
The capers that he cut up when the circus come to town;
How the old ringmaster nagged him; all his frolics an' his fuss,
Jest the best thing in the circus—was the old-time circus clown
    to us.

When he smiled we fell to laughin'; when he laughed we gave
    a shout;
We was always watchin' for him and a-follerin' about;
He used to come so reg'lar that we knowed him up and down,
He was sociable an' friendly—was the old-time circus clown.

We would jump behind his wagon when he wasn't telling jokes,
An' he'd give a grin o' welcome; maybe ask us how's the folks;
He knowed the little boys and girls from Billville to Brown
An' they loved him every one o' them—the old-time circus
clown.

I wonder where he's gone to now? The circus comes along,
An' the steam pianer's playing of a screetchy sort o' song.
There's half a dozen painted chaps in every street parade,
But their fun is mighty solemn to the fun the old clown made.

I wonder what's become o' him? I guess they've laid him by;
Warn't use to three-ringed circuses an' women kickin' high,
He kinder saw his time was up; the circus lights growed dim,
An' he couldn't see the faces of the old boys cheerin' him.

He's gone, an' gone forever, but on every circus day,
When I sit with all the children where the new clowns play,
My old eyes grow right misty, an' a tear comes tumblin' down
From an old-time circus feller for the old-time circus clown.

A Bird in the Hand Is Worth Two in the Bush

There are two little songsters, well known in the land,
  Their names are I-Have and O-Had-I;
I-Have will come tamely and perch on your hand,
  But O-Had-I will mock you most sadly.

I-Have, at first sight, is less fair to the eye,
  But his worth is by far more enduring
Than a thousand O-Had-I's, that sit far and high
  On roofs and on trees so alluring.

Full many a golden egg this bird will lay,
  And sing you, "Be cheery! Be cherry!"
O merrily then will the day glide away,
  And sweet shall your sleep be when weary.

But let an O-Had-I but once take your eye,
  And a longing to catch him once seize you,
He'll give you no comfort nor rest till you die —
  Life-long he'll torment you and tease you.

He'll keep you all day running up and down hill,
  Now racing, now panting and creeping;
While far overland this sweet bird at his will,
  With his bright golden plumage, is sweeping.

Then every wise man who attends to my song
  Will count his I-Have a choice treasure,
And where'er an O-Had-I comes flying along,
  Will just let him fly at his pleasure.

Items

of

Unusual

Interest

Class of '68, as seen by '18

by John S. Knight

From *The Chicago Daily News*, June 22, 1968

It was my recent privilege to visit two great universities, Cornell and Harvard.

My own Cornell class of 1918 proved its durability by having the largest reunion attendance on the campus. This over-70 group had survived two world wars, the Depression and a plethora of plaguing problems, public and personal.

But it was my grandson and the other young men of 1968 at Harvard who interested me most and with whom I shared the most liquid and intellectual stimulation.

When parents and grandparents try to judge the youth of today by their standards of yesteryear, we have an immediate generation gap.

The inability to understand the motivations, sensitivities and convictions of our younger people only widens the chasm.

Nothing is as simple to them as it was to us. This generation cannot grasp or accept that the Vietnam war is a holy crusade against communism.

They see it as an immoral war in which we kill people for whom we have no dislike, burn villages and cities to "save them," destroy and inflict misery upon civilian populations who seek only to live a peaceful life.

The class of 1968 is deeply involved in the great issues of today. Its members mistrust politicians, the press and the President.

They are wary of the "work hard and succeed" formula for advancement. Whereas the student of the 1950's was accused of too much conformism and complacency, the student of the mid-1960's is best described by President James A. Perkins of Cornell as "independent, restless, antiauthoritarian, concerned and sometimes a little frightened."

He regards himself, says Perkins, as "a citizen first and a student second. For him the notion of study for the sake of study has been replaced by a demand that knowledge have relevance to today. If they cannot find relevance in their courses of study, they will find it in social or political action."

The flocking of students to Senator Eugene McCarthy is a manifestation of this restlessness and concern. They have little sympathy with either President Johnson or the two probable presidential candidates, Richard Nixon and Hubert Humphrey.

Admittedly, the class of 1968 has some extremely fuzzy views about economics and the workings of our profit-and-loss system. This is largely attributable to the teachings of university theorists who have but a modicum of exposure to the system itself.

Yet these young men made a profound impression upon me.

Whereas their elders often succumb to a rigidity of thought, the class of 1968 refuses to accept old dogmas. The educated young man or woman of today is searching for a better tomorrow, not for himself or herself alone but for the world and its peoples.

And even from those who brought about so much turmoil in the colleges may come the strongest and most thoughtful leaders of tomorrow as they acquire a balance of individual freedom and social responsibility.

After days of conversations I came away with a badly deflated ego from the realization of how little I knew at a comparable age.

June

by James Whitcomb Riley

O queenly month of indolent repose!
I drink thy breath in sips of rare perfume,
    As in thy downy lap of clover-bloom
I nestle like a drowsy child, and doze
The lazy hours away. The zephyr throws
    The shifting shuttle of the summer's loom,
    And weaves a damask-work of gleam and gloom
Before thy listless feet: the lily blows
    A bugle-call of fragrance o'er the glade;
        And, wheeling into ranks, with plume and spear,
    Thy harvest-armies gather on parade;
        While, faint and far away, yet pure and clear,
A voice calls out of alien lands of shade,—
    "All hail the Peerless Goddess of the Year!"

Problems of the Past Resemble the Present

A few comments made by Franklin D. Roosevelt
at various periods of his trying times

Doctrines which set group against group, faith against faith, race against race, class against class, fanning the fires of hatred in men too despondent, too desperate to think for themselves, were used as rabble-rousing slogans on which dictators could rise to power. And once in power they could saddle their tyrannies on whole nations, saddle them on weaker neighbors.

This is the danger to which we in America must begin to be more alert. For the apologists for foreign aggressors, and equally those selfish and partisan groups at home who wrap themselves in a false mantle of Americanism to promote their own economic, financial or political advantage, are now trying European tricks upon us, seeking to muddy the stream of our national thinking, weakening us in the face of danger, by trying to set our own people to fighting among themselves. Such tactics are what have helped to plunge Europe into war. We must combat them, as we would the plague, if American integrity and security are to be preserved. We cannot afford to face the future as a disunited people.

We must as a united people keep ablaze on this continent the flames of human liberty, of reason, of democracy, and of fair play as living things to be preserved for the better world that is to come.

Annual Message to Congress
January 3, 1940

Today we seek a moral basis for peace. It cannot be a real peace if it fails to recognize brotherhood. It cannot be a lasting peace if the fruit of it is oppression, or starvation, or cruelty, or human life dominated by armed camps. It cannot be a sound peace if small nations must live in fear of powerful neighbors. It cannot be a moral peace if freedom from invasion is sold for tribute. It cannot be an intelligent peace if it denies free passage to that knowledge of those ideals which permit men to find common ground. It cannot be a righteous peace if worship of God is denied.

Radio Address
March 16, 1940

These unhappy times call for the building of plans that rest upon the forgotten, the unorganized but the indispensable units of economic power, for plans like those of 1917 that build from the bottom up and not from the top down, that put their faith once more in the forgotten man at the bottom of the economic pyramid.

Radio Address, Albany, N. Y.
April 7, 1932

The country needs and, unless I mistake its temper, the country demands bold, persistent experimentation. It is common sense to take a method and try it. If it fails, admit it frankly and try another. But above all, try something. The millions who are in want will not stand by silently forever while the things to satisfy their needs are within easy reach.

We need enthusiasm, imagination and the ability to face facts, even unpleasant ones, bravely. We need to correct, by drastic means if necessary, the faults in our economic system from which we now suffer. We need the courage of the young. Yours is not the task of making your way in the world, but the task of remaking the world which you will find before you. May every one of us be granted the courage, the faith and the vision to give the best that is in us to that remaking!

Address at Oglethorpe University
May 22, 1932

When it comes to baseball I am the kind of fan who wants to get plenty of action for his money. I have some appreciation of a game which is featured by a pitcher's duel and results in a score of one to nothing. But I must confess that I get the biggest kick out of the biggest score—a game in which the batters pole the ball into the far corners of the field, the outfielders scramble, and men run the bases. In short, my idea of the best game is one that guarantees the fans a combined score of not less than fifteen runs, divided about eight to seven.

Franklin D. Roosevelt
January 23, 1937

The Age Has Great Tasks

by Theodore Roosevelt

(circa 1900)

We of this generation do not have to face a task such as that our fathers faced, but we have our tasks, and woe to us if we fail to perform them! We cannot, if we would, play the part of China, and be content to rot by inches in ignoble ease within our borders, taking no interest in what goes on beyond them; sunk in a scrambling commercialism; heedless of the higher life, the life of aspiration, of toil and risk; busying ourselves only with the wants of our bodies for the day; until suddenly we should find, beyond a shadow of question, what China has already found, that in this world the nation that has trained itself to a career of unwarlike and isolated ease is bound in the end to go down before other nations which have not lost the manly and adventurous qualities.

If we are to be a really great people, we must strive in good faith to play a great part in the world. We cannot avoid meeting great issues. All that we can determine for ourselves is whether we shall meet them well or ill. Last year we could not help being brought face to face with the problem of war with Spain. All we could decide was whether we should shirk like cowards from the contest or enter into it as beseemed a brave and high-spirited people; and, once in, whether failure or success should crown our banners. So it is now.

We cannot avoid the responsibilities that confront us in Hawaii, Cuba, Puerto Rico, and the Philippines. All we can decide is whether we shall meet them in a way that will redound to the national credit, or whether we shall make of our dealings with these new problems a dark and shameful page in our history. To refuse to deal with them at all merely amounts to dealing with them badly. We have a given problem to solve. If we undertake the solution, there is, of course, always danger that we may not solve it aright, but to refuse to undertake the solution simply renders it certain that we cannot possibly serve it aright.

"Heaven smiled upon and gave us liberty and independence"

Some thoughts by Andrew Jackson that are worth pondering, as expressed in a letter to Dr. L. H. Colman.

Sir: I have had the honor this day to receive your letter of the 21st instant, and with candor shall reply to it. My name has been brought before the nation by the people themselves without any agency of mine: for I wish it not to be forgotten that I have never solicited office, nor when called upon by the constituted authorities have ever declined—where I conceived my services would be beneficial to my country. As my name has been brought before the nation for the first office in the gift of the people, it is incumbent on me, when asked, frankly to declare my opinion upon any political or national question pending before and about which the country feels an interest.

You ask me my opinion on the Tariff. I answer, that I am in favor of a judicious examination and revision of it; and so far as the Tariff before us embraces the design of fostering, protecting, and preserving within ourselves the means of national defense and independence, particularly in a state of war, I would advocate it and support it. The experience of the late war ought to teach us a lesson; and one never to be forgotten. If our liberty and republican form of government, procured for us by our Revolutionary fathers, are worth the blood and treasure at which they were obtained, it surely is our duty to protect and defend them. Can there be an American patriot, who saw the privations, dangers, and difficulties experienced for the want of a proper means of defense during the last war, who would be willing again to hazard the safety of our country if embroiled; or rest it for defense on the precarious means of national resources to be derived from commerce, in a state of war with a maritime power which might destroy that commerce to prevent our obtaining the means of defense, and thereby subdue us? I hope there is not; and if there is, I am sure he does not deserve to enjoy the blessings of freedom.

Heaven smiled upon and gave us liberty and independence. That same Providence has blessed us with the means of national independence and national defense. If we omit or refuse to use the gifts which He has extended to us, we deserve not the continuation of His blessings. He has filled our mountains and our plains with minerals—with lead, iron, and copper, and given us a climate and a soil for the growing of hemp and wool. These being the grand materials of our national defense, they ought to have extended to them adequate and fair protection, that our own manufactories and laborers may be placed on a fair competition with those of Europe; and that we may have within our own country a supply of those leading and important articles so essential to war. Beyond this, I look at the Tariff with an eye to the proper distribution of labor and revenue; and with a view to discharge our national debt. I am one of those who do not believe that a national debt is a national blessing, but rather a curse to a republic; inasmuch as it is calculated to raise around the administration a moneyed aristocracy dangerous to the liberties of the country.

This Tariff—I mean a judicious one—possesses more fanciful than real dangers. I will ask what is the real situation of the agriculturalist? Where has the American farmer a market for his surplus products? Except for cotton he has neither a foreign nor a home market. Does not this clearly prove, when there is no market either at home or abroad, that there is too much labor employed in agriculture – and that the channels of labor should be multiplied? Common sense points out at once the remedy. Draw from agriculture the superabundant labor, employ it in mechanism and manufactures, thereby creating a home market for your breadstuffs, and distributing labor to a most profitable account, and benefits to the country will result. Take from agriculture in the United States six hundred thousand men, women, and children, and you at once give a home market for more breadstuffs than all Europe now furnishes us. In short, sir, we have been too long subject to the policy of the British merchants. It is time we should become a little more *Americanized*, and instead of feeding the paupers and laborers of Europe, feed our own, or else in a short time, by continuing our present policy, we shall all be paupers ourselves.

It is, therefore, my opinion that a careful Tariff is much wanted to pay our national debt, and afford us a means of that defense within ourselves on which the safety and liberty of our country depend; and last, though not least, to our labor, which must prove beneficial to the happiness, independence, and wealth of the community.

This is a short outline of my opinions, generally, on the subject of your inquiry, and believing them correct and calculated to further the prosperity and happiness of my country, I declare to you I would not barter them for any office or situation of temporal character that could be given me. I have presented you my opinions freely, because I am without concealment, and should indeed despise myself if I could believe myself capable of acquiring the confidence of any by means so ignoble.

Afterwhiles

by James Whitcomb Riley

Where are they—the Afterwhiles—
Luring us the lengthening miles
Of our lives? Where is the dawn
With the dew across the lawn
Stroked with eager feet the far
Way the hills and valleys are?
Where the sun that smites the frown
Of the eastward-gazer down?
Where the rifted wreathes of mist
O'er us, tinged with amethyst,
Round the mountain's steep defiles?
Where are all the afterwhiles?

Afterwhile—and we will go
Thither, yon, and to and fro—
From the stifling city-streets
To the country's cool retreats—
From the riot to the rest
Where hearts beat the placidest;
Afterwhile, and we will fall
Under breezy trees, and loll
In the shade, with thirsty sight
Drinking deep the blue delight
Of the skies that will beguile
Us as children—afterwhile.

Afterwhile—and one intends
To be gentler to his friends—
To walk with them, in the hush
Of still evenings, o'er the plush
Of home-leading fields, and stand
Long at parting, hand in hand:
One, in time, will joy to take
New resolves for someone's sake,
And wear then the look that lies
Clear and pure in other eyes—
He will soothe and reconcile
His own conscience—afterwhile.

Afterwhile—we have in view
A far scene to journey to,—
Where the old home is, and where
The old mother waits us there,
Peering, as the time grows late,
Down the old path to the gate.—
How we'll click the latch that locks
In the pinks and hollyhocks,
And leap up the path once more
Where she waits us at the door!—
How we'll greet the dear old smile,
And the warm tears—afterwhile!

Ah, the endless afterwhiles!—
Leagues on leagues, and miles on miles,
In the distance far withdrawn,
Stretching on, and on, and on,
Till the fancy is footsore
And faints in the dust before
The last milestone's granite face,
Hacked with: Here Beginneth Space.
O far glimmering worlds and wings,
Mystic smiles and beckonings,
Lead us, through the shadowy aisles,
Out into the afterwhiles.

There Is a Better Weapon than the H-Bomb

An excerpt from a speech by President John F. Kennedy before the United Nations, September 20, 1963.

The task of building the peace lies with the leaders of every nation, large and small. For the great powers have no monopoly on conflict or ambition. The Cold War is not the only expression of tension in this world, and the nuclear race is not the only arms race. Even little wars are dangerous in a nuclear world. The long labor of peace is an undertaking for every nation, and in this effort none of us can remain unaligned. To this goal none can be uncommitted.

The reduction of global tension must not be an excuse for the narrow pursuit of self-interest. If the Soviet Union and the United States, with all their global interests and clashing commitments of ideology, and with nuclear weapons still aimed at each other today, can find areas of common interest and agreement, then surely other nations can do the same— nations caught in regional conflicts, in racial issues or in the death throes of old colonialism. Chronic disputes which divert precious resources from the needs of the people or drain the energies of both sides serve the interests of no one, and the badge of responsibility in the modern world is a willingness to seek peaceful solutions.

It is never too early to try; and it is never too late to talk; and it is high time that many disputes on the agenda of this Assembly were taken off the debating schedule and placed on the negotiating table.

The fact remains that the United States, as a major nuclear power, does have a special responsibility in the world. It is, in fact, a threefold responsibility: a responsibility to our own citizens, a responsibility to the people of the whole world who are affected by our decisions, and to the next generation of humanity. We believe the Soviet Union also has these special responsibilities, and that those responsibilities require our two nations to concentrate less on our differences and more on the means of resolving them peacefully. For too long both of us have increased our military budgets, our nuclear stockpiles and our capacity to destroy all life—human, animal, vegetable— without any corresponding increase in our security.

Our conflicts, to be sure, are real. Our concepts of the world are different. No service is performed by failing to make clear our disagreements. A central difference is the belief of the American people in self-determination for all people.

We believe that the people of Germany and Berlin must be free to reunite their capital and their country.

We believe that the people of Cuba must be free to secure the fruits of the revolution that has been betrayed from within and exploited from without.

In short, we believe that in all the world—in Eastern Europe as well as Western, in Southern Africa as well as Northern, in old nations as well as new—people must be free to choose their own future, without discrimination or dictation, without coercion or subversion.

These are the basic differences between the Soviet Union and the United States, and they cannot be concealed. So long as they exist, they set limits to agreement, and they forbid the relaxation of our vigilance. Our defense around the world will be maintained for the protection of freedom, and our determination to safeguard that freedom will measure up to any threat or challenge.

But I would say to the leaders of the Soviet Union, and to their people, that if either of our countries is to be fully secure, we need a much better weapon than the H-bomb, a weapon better than ballistic missiles or nuclear submarines, and that better weapon is peaceful cooperation.

Former Soviet Russian Premier Nikita S. Khrushchev and the late President John F. Kennedy in Vienna, Austria, June 4, 1961.

Spiritual Comforts Only in the Early Years of New England Church History

From *The Sabbath in Puritan New England* by ALICE MORSE EARLE

The first church of Salem built a "cattied chimney twelve feet long" in its meeting-house in 1662, but five years later it was removed, perhaps through the colonists' dread lest the building be destroyed by a conflagration caused by the combustible nature of the materials of which the chimney was composed. Felt, in his "Annals of Salem," asserts that the First Church of Boston was the first New England congregation to have a stove for heating the meeting-house at the time of public worship; this was in 1773. This statement is incorrect. Mr. Judd says the Hadley church had an iron stove in their meeting-house as early as 1734—the Hadley people were such sybarites and novelty-lovers in those early days! The Old South Church of Boston followed in the luxurious fashion in 1783, and the "Evening Post" of January 25, 1783, contained a poem of which these four lines show the criticising and deprecating spirit:—

> Extinct the sacred fire of love,
> Our zeal grown cold and dead,
> In the house of God we fix a stove
> To warm us in their stead.

Other New England congregations piously froze during service-time well into this century. The Longmeadow church, early in the field, had a stove in 1810; the Salem people in 1815; and the Medford meeting in 1820. The church in Brimfield in 1819 refused to pay for a stove, but ordered as some sacrifice to the desire for comfort, two extra doors placed on the gallery-stairs to keep out draughts; but when in that town, a few years later, a subscription was made to buy a church stove, one old member refused to contribute, saying "good preaching kept him hot enough without stoves."

As all the church edifices were built without any thought of the possibility of such comfortable furniture, they had to be adapted as best they might to the ungainly and unsightly great stoves which were usually placed in the central aisle of the building. From these cast-iron monsters, there extended to the nearest windows and projected through them, hideous stove-pipes that too often spread, from every leaky and ill-fastened joint, smoke and sooty vapors, and sometimes pyroligneous drippings on the congregation. Often tin pails to catch the drippings were hung under the stove-pipes, forming a further chaste and elegant church-decoration. Many serious objections were made to the stoves besides the æsthetic ones. It was alleged that they would be the means of starting many destructive conflagrations; that they caused severe headaches in the church attendants; and worst of all, that the *heat warped the ladies' tortoise-shell back-combs.*

The church reformers contended, on the other hand, that no one could properly receive spiritual comfort while enduring such decided bodily discomfort. They hoped that with increased physical warmth, fervor in religion would be equally augmented,— that, as Cowper wrote,—

> The churches warmed, they would no longer hold
> Such frozen figures, stiff as they are cold.

Many were the quarrels and discussions that arose in New England communities over the purchase and use of stoves, and many were the meetings held and votes taken upon the important subject.

"Peter Parley"— Mr. Samuel Goodrich — gave, in his "Recollections," a very amusing account of the sufferings endured by the wife of an anti-stove deacon. She came to church with a look of perfect resignation on the Sabbath of the stove's introduction, and swept past the unwelcome intruder with averted head, and into her pew. She sat there through the service, growing paler with the unaccustomed heat, until the minister's words about "heaping coals of fire" brought too keen a sense of the overwhelming and unhealthful stove-heat to her mind, and she fainted. She was carried out of church, and upon recovering said languidly that it "was the heat from the stove." A most complete and sudden resuscitation was effected, however, when she was informed of the fact that no fire had as yet been lighted in the new church-furnishing.

Similar chronicles exist about other New England churches, and bear a striking resemblance to each other. Rev. Henry Ward Beecher in an address delivered in New York on December 20, 1853, the anniversary of the Landing of the Pilgrims, referred to the opposition made to the introduction of stoves into the old meeting-house in Litchfield, Connecticut, during the ministry of his father, and gave an amusing account of the results of the introgression. This allusion called up many reminiscences of anti-stove wars, and a writer in the "New York Enquirer" told the same story of the fainting woman in Litchfield meeting, who began to fan herself and at length swooned, saying when she recovered "that the heat of the horrid stove had caused her to faint." A correspondent of the "Cleveland Herald" confirmed the fact that the fainting episode occurred in the Litchfield meeting-house. The editor of the "Hartford Daily Courant" thus added his testimony: —

"Violent opposition had been made to the introduction of a stove in the old meeting-house, and an attempt made in vain to induce the society to purchase one. The writer was one of seven young men who finally purchased a stove and requested permission to put it up in the meeting-house on trial. After much difficulty the committee consented. It was all arranged on Saturday afternoon, and on Sunday we took our seats in the Bass, rather earlier than usual, to see the fun. It was a warm November Sunday, in which the sun shone cheerfully and warmly on the old south steps and into the naked windows. The stove stood in the middle aisle, rather in front of the Tenor Gallery. People came in and stared. Good old Deacon Trowbridge, one of the most simple-hearted and worthy men of that generation, had, as Mr. Beecher says, been induced to give up his opposition. He shook his head, however, as he felt the heat reflected from it, and gathered up the skirts of his great coat as he passed up the broad aisle to the deacon's seat. Old Uncle Noah Stone, a wealthy farmer of the West End, who sat near, scowled and muttered at the effects of the heat, but waited until noon to utter his maledictions over his nut-cakes and cheese at the intermission. There had in fact been *no fire in the stove,* the day being too warm. We were too much upon the broad grin to be very devotional, and smiled rather loudly at the funny things we saw. But when the editor of the village paper, Mr. Bunce, came in (who was a believer in stoves in churches) and with a most satisfactory air warmed his hands by the stove, keeping the skirts of his great-coat carefully between his knees, we could stand it no longer but dropped invisible behind the breastwork. But the climax of the whole was (as the Cleveland man says) when Mrs. Peck went out in the middle of the service. It was, however, the means of reconciling the whole society; for after that first day we heard no more opposition to the warm stove in the meeting-house."

With all this corroborative evidence I think it is fully proved that the event really happened in Litchfield, and that the honor was stolen for other towns by unveracious chroniclers; otherwise we must believe in an amazing unanimity of church-joking and sham-fainting all over New England.

The very nature, the stern, pleasure-hating and trial-glorying Puritan nature, which made our forefathers leave their English homes to come, for the love of God and the freedom of conscience, to these wild, barren, and unwelcoming shores, made them also endure with fortitude and almost with satisfaction all personal discomforts, and caused them to cling with persistent firmness to such outward symbols of austere contempt of luxury, and such narrow-minded signs of love of simplicity as the lack of comfortable warmth during the time of public worship. The religion which they had endured such bitter hardships to establish, did not, in their minds, need any shielding and coddling to keep it alive, but thrived far better on Spartan severity and simplicity; hence, it took two centuries of gradual and most tardy softening and modifying of character to prepare the Puritan mind for so advanced a reform and luxury as proper warmth in the meeting-houses in winter.

* * * * *

For many years after the settlement of New England the Puritans, even in outwardly tranquil times, went armed to meeting; and to sanctify the Sunday gun-loading they were expressly forbidden to fire off their charges at any object on that day save an Indian or a wolf, their two "greatest inconveniencies." Trumbull, in his "Mac Fingal," writes thus in jest of this custom of Sunday arm-bearing:—

> So once, for fear of Indian beating,
> Our grandsires bore their guns to meeting,—
> Each man equipped on Sunday morn
> With psalm-book, shot, and powder-horn,
> And looked in form, as all must grant,
> Like the ancient true church militant.

* * * * *

An old gentleman, lamenting the razing of the church of his childhood, told the story of his youthful Sabbaths in rhyme, and thus refers with affectionate enthusiasm to the old custom of bringing bunches of esculent "sallet" herbs to meeting:—

> And when I tired and restless grew,
> Our next pew neighbor, Mrs. True,
> Reached her kind hand the top rail through
> To hand me dill, and fennel too,
> And sprigs of caraway.

And as I munched the spicy seeds,
I dimly felt that kindly deeds
That thus supply our present needs,
Though only gifts of pungent weeds,
Show true religion.

And often now through sermon trite
And operatic singer's flight,
I long for that old friendly sight,
The hand with herbs of value light,
To help to pass the time.

Were the dill and "sweetest fennel" chosen Sabbath favorites
for their old-time virtues and powers?

"Vervain and dill
Hinder witches of their ill."

Sleep

by JAMES WHITCOMB RILEY

Orphaned, I cry to thee,
Sweet sleep: O, kneel and be
A mother unto me!
    Calm thou my childish fears,
And fold mine eyelids to all tenderly,
    And dry my tears.

Come, Sleep, all drowsy-eyed
And faint with languor, slide
Thy dim face down beside
    Mine own, that I may rest
And nestle in thine arms and there abide
    And be thy guest.

Good night to every care,
And shadow of despair—
Good night to all things where
    Within is no delight!—
Sleep opens her dark arms, and swooning
        there
    I cry, Good night!

Our Enemy, the Cat

by ALAN DEVOE

From *Down to Earth: A Naturalist Looks About*
Copyright 1937, 1938, 1939, 1940 by Alan Devoe
Published by Coward McCann, Inc.

We tie bright ribbons around their necks, and occasionally little tinkling bells, and we affect to think that they are as sweet and vapid as the coy name "kitty" by which we call them would imply. It is a curious illusion. For, purring beside our fireplaces and pattering along our back fences, we have got a wild beast as uncowed and uncorrupted as any under heaven.

It is five millenniums since we snared the wild horse and broke his spirit to our whim, and for centuries beyond counting we have been able to persuade the once-free dog to fawn and cringe and lick our hands. But a man must be singularly blind with vanity to fancy that in the three—ten?—thousand years during which we have harbored cats beneath our roof-trees, we have succeeded in reducing them to any such insipid estate. It is not a "pet" (that most degraded of creatures) that we have got in our house, whatever we may like to think. It is a wild beast; and there adheres to its sleek fur no smallest hint of the odor of humanity.

It would be a salutary thing if those who write our simpering verses and tales about "tabby-sit-by-the-fire" could bring themselves to see her honestly, to look into her life with eyes unblurred by wishful sentiment. It would be a good thing — to start at the beginning—to follow her abroad into the moonlight on one of those raw spring evenings when the first skunk-cabbages are thrusting their veined tips through the melting snow and when the loins of catdom are hot with lust.

The love-play of domestic creatures is mostly a rather comic thing, and loud are the superior guffaws of rustic humans to see the clumsy, fumbling antics that take place in the kennels and the stockpen. But the man had better not laugh who sees cats in their rut. He is looking upon something very like aboriginal passion, untainted by any of the overlaid refinements, suppressions, and modifications that have been acquired by most of mankind's beasts. The mating of cats has neither the bathetic clumsiness of dogs' nor the lumbering ponderous-

ness of cattle's, but—conducted in a lonely secret place, away from human view—is marked by a quick concentrated intensity of lust that lies not far from the border-line of agony. The female, in the tense moment of the prelude, tears with her teeth at her mate's throat, and, as the climax of the creatures' frenzy comes, the lean silky-furred flanks quiver vibrantly as a taut wire. Then quietly, in the spring night, the two beasts go their ways.

It will be usually May before the kittens come; and that episode, too, will take place secretly, in its ancient feline fashion, where no maudlin human eye may see. Great is the pique in many a house when "pussy," with dragging belly and distended dugs, disappears one night—scorning the cushioned maternity-bed that has been prepared for her—and creeps on silent feet to the dankest cranny of the cellar, there in decent aloneness to void her blood and babies. She does not care, any more than a lynx does, or a puma, to be pried upon while she licks the birth-hoods from her squirming progeny and cleans away the membrane with her rough pink tongue.

A kitten is not a pretty thing at birth. For many days it is a wriggling mite of lumpy flesh and sinew, blind and unaware, making soft sucking noises with its wet, toothless mouth, and smelling of milk. Daily, hourly, the rough tongue of the tabby ministers to it in its helplessness, glossing the baby-fur with viscid spittle, licking away the uncontrolled dung, cleaning away the crumbly pellet of dried blood from its pointed ears. By that tenth or fourteenth day when its eyes wholly unseal, blue and weak in their newness, the infant cat is clean to immaculateness, and an inalienable fastidiousness is deep-lodged in its spirit.

It is now—when the kitten makes its first rushes and sallies from its birthplace, and, with extraordinary gymnastics of its chubby body, encounters chair-legs and human feet and other curious phenomena—that it elicits from man those particular expressions of gurgling delight which we reserve for very tiny fluffy creatures who act very comically. But the infant cat has no coy intent to be amusing. If he is comic, it is only because of the incongruity of so demure a look and so wild a heart. For in that furry head of his, grim and ancient urges are already dictating.

Hardly larger than a powder-puff, he crouches on the rug and watches a fleck of lint. His little blue eyes are bright, and presently his haunches tense and tremble. The tiny body shivers in an ague of excitement. He pounces, a little clumsily perhaps, and pinions the fleeting lint-fleck with his paws. In the fractional second of that lunge, the ten small needles of his claws have shot from their sheaths of flesh and muscle. It is a good game; but it is not an idle one. It is the kitten's introduction into the ancient ritual of the kill. Those queer little stiff-legged rushes and prancings are the heritage of an old death-dance, and those jerkings of his hind legs, as he rolls on his back, are the preparation for that day when—in desperate conflict with a bigger beast than himself—he will win the fight by the time-old feline technique of disembowelment. Even now, in his early infancy, he is wholly and inalienably a cat.

While he is still young he has already formulated his attitude toward the human race into whose midst he has been born. It is an attitude not easily described, but compounded of a great pride, a great reserve, a towering integrity. It is even to be fancied that there is something in it of a sort of bleak contempt. Solemnly the cat watches these great hulking two-legged creatures into whose strange tribe he has unaccountably been born—and who are so clumsy, so noisy, so vexing to his quiet spirit—and in his feline heart is neither love nor gratitude. He learns to take the food which they give him, to relish the warmth and the comfort and the caresses which they can

offer, but these profferments do not persuade his wild mis-
trustful heart to surrender itself. He will not sell himself, as a
dog will, for a scrap of meat; he will not enter into an allegiance.
He is unchangeably and incorruptibly a cat, and he will accommodate himself to the ways and spirit of mankind no more
than the stern necessity of his unnatural environment requires.

II

Quietly he dozes by the fire or on a lap, and purrs in his happiness because he loves the heat. But let him choose to move,
and if any human hand tries to restrain him for more than a
moment he will struggle and unsheathe his claws and lash out
with a furious hate. Let a whip touch him and he will slink off
in a sullen fury, uncowed and outraged and unrepenting. For
the things which man gives to him are not so precious or essential that he will trade them for his birthright, which is the right
to be himself—a furred four-footed being of ancient lineage,
loving silence and aloneness and the night, and esteeming the
smell of rat's blood above any possible human excellence.

He may live for perhaps ten years; occasionally even for
twenty. Year after year he drinks the daily milk that is put
faithfully before him, dozes in laps whose contours please him,
accepts with casual pleasure the rubbing of human fingers
under his chin—and withdraws, in every significant hour of his
life, as far away from human society as he is able. Far from
the house, in a meadow or a woods if he can find one, he
crouches immobile for hours, his lithe body flattened conceal-
ingly in the grass or ferns, and waits for prey.

With a single pounce he can break a rabbit's spine as though
it were a brittle twig. When he has caught a tawny meadow-
mouse or a mole, he has, too, the ancient cat-ecstasy of toying
and playing with it, letting it die slowly, in a long agony, for
his amusement. Sometimes, in a dim remembrance from the
remote past of his race, he may bring home his kill; but mostly
he returns to the house as neat and demure as when he left,
with his chops licked clean of blood.

Immaculate, unobtrusive, deep withdrawn into himself, he
passes through the long years of his enforced companionship
with humanity. He takes from his masters (how absurd a word
it is) however much they may care to give him; of himself he
surrenders nothing. However often he be decked with ribbons

and cuddled and petted and made much over, his cold pride never grows less, and his grave calm gaze—tinged perhaps with a gentle distaste—is never lighted by adoration. To the end he adores only his own gods, the gods of mating, of hunting, and of the lonely darkness.

One day, often with no forewarning whatever, he is gone from the house and never returns. He has felt the presaging shadow of death, and he goes to meet it in the old unchanging way of the wild—alone. A cat does not want to die with the smell of humanity in his nostrils and the noise of humanity in his delicate peaked ears. Unless death strikes very quickly and suddenly, he creeps away to where it is proper that a proud wild beast should die—not on one of man's rugs or cushions, but in a lonely quiet place, with his muzzle pressed against the cold earth.

Twenty Cats add up to *Catastrophe*

From George Cruikshank's *Omnibus*

A *cat* I sing, of famous memory,
Though *cat*achrestical my song may be;
In a small garden *cat*acomb she lies,
And *cat*aclysms fill her comrades' eyes;
Borne on the air, the *cat*acoustic song
Swells with her virtues' *cat*alogue along;
No *cat*aplasm could lengthen out her years,
Though mourning friends shed *cat*aracts of tears
Once loud and strong her *cat*echist-like voice
It dwindled to a *cat*call's squeaking noise;
Most *cat*egorical her virtues shone,
By *cat*enation join'd each one to one;—
But a vile *cat*chpoll dog, with cruel bite,
Like *cat*ling's cut, her strength disabled quite;
Her *cat*erwauling pierced the heavy air,
As *cat*aphracts their arms through legions bear;
'Tis vain! as *cat*erpillars drag away
Their lengths, like *cat*tle after busy day,
She ling'ring died, nor left in kit *k*at the
Embodyment of this *cat*astrophe.

Indian Life and Lore

One of the earliest descriptions of the American Indian

From *Plain Dealing* by THOMAS LECHFORD

They are of body tall, proper, and straight. They go naked, save about their middle. Seldom are they abroad in the extremity of winter, but keep in their wigwams till necessity drives them forth; and then they wrap themselves in skins, or some of our English coarse cloth; and for the winter they have boots, or a kind of laced, tawed-leather stockings.

They are naturally proud, and idle, given much to singing, dancing, and plays. They are governed by Sachems, Kings; and Sagamores, petty Lords; by an absolute tyranny.

Their women are of comely features, industrious, and do most of the labor in planting and the carrying of burdens. Their husbands hold them in great slavery, yet never knowing otherwise, it is the less grievous to them. They say, "Englishman much fool, for spoiling good working creatures," meaning women. And when they see any of our English women sewing with their needles or working coifs, or such things, they will cry out, "Lazy squaws!" But they are much the kinder to their wives by the example of the English.

Their children they will not part with upon any terms, to be taught. They are of complexion swarthy and tawny. Their children are born white, but they bedaub them with oil and colors, presently. All that I saw have black hair.

In times of mourning, they paint their faces with black lead —black all about the eyebrows and on part of their cheeks. In time of rejoicing, they paint red, with a kind of vermilion.

They cut their hair in divers forms, according to their nation or people, so that you may know a tribe by its cut; and ever they have a long lock on one side of their heads, and wear feathers of peacocks, and such like, and red cloth or ribands at their locks; beads of wampumpeag about their necks, and a girdle of the same, wrought with blue and white wampum after the manner of checker work, two fingers broad, about their loins. Some of their chief men wear pendants of wampum and such toys in their ears, and some of the chief women wear fair bracelets and chains of wampum. Such men and women come confidently among the English.

Since the Pequot War they are kept in very good subjection and held to strict points of justice, so that the English may work safely among them. But the French in the East, and the

Dutch in the South, sell them guns, powder and shot.

They have Powwows, or Priests, who are Witches, and a kind of Chirurgion [surgeon], but some of them, notwithstanding, are fain to be beholden to the English Chirurgions. They have their times of powwowing, which, of late, they have called prayers, according to the English word. The Powwow labors himself in his incantations to extreme sweating and weariness, even to ecstasy. The Powwows cannot work their witchcrafts if any of the English be by; neither can any of their incantations lay hold on, or do any harm to, the English, as I have been credibly informed. The Powwow is next to the King, or Sachem, and commonly when he dies, the Powwow marries the Squaw Sachem, that is, the Queen.

They have marriages among them; they have many wives; they say, they commit much filthiness among themselves. But for every marriage, the Sagamore has a fathom of wampum, which is about seven or eight shillings in value. Some of them will diligently attend to anything they can understand by any of our religion, and are very willing to teach their language to any English.

They live much the better, and peaceably, because of the English; and they know it—or at least their Sachems and Sagamores know so much—for before, they did nothing but spoil and destroy one another.

They live in wigwams, or houses made of mats, like little huts, the fire in the midst of the house. They cut down a tree with axes and hatchets, bought of the English, Dutch, or French, and bring the butt-end into the wigwam upon the hearth, and so burn it by degrees.

They live upon parched corn, which, of late, they grind at our English mills, venison, beavers, otters, oysters, clams, lobsters, and other fish, ground-nuts, and acorns, which they boil all together in a kettle.

Their riches are their wampum, bowls, trays, kettles, and spoons, beaver, furs, and canoes. He is a Sachem whose wife has her clean spoons in a chest, for some chief Englishmen, when they come as guests to the wigwam.

They lie upon a mat, with a stone or a piece of wood under their heads. They will give the best entertainment they can make to any English coming amongst them. They will not taste sweet things, nor alter their habit willingly; only they are taken with tobacco, wine, and strong waters; and I have seen some of them in English or French clothes.

Their ordinary weapons are bows and arrows, and long staves, or half pikes, with pieces of swords, daggers, or knives in the ends of them. They have Captains, and are very good at a short mark, and nimble of foot to run away. Their manner of fighting is, most commonly, all in one file.

They are many in number and worship Kitan, their good god, or Hobbamocco, their evil god; but more fear Hobbamocco, because he does them most harm.

Among some of these nations, their policy is to have two Kings at a time, but, I think, of one family; the one aged for counsel, the other younger for action. Their Kings succeed by inheritance.

Master Henry Dunster, schoolmaster of Cambridge, deserves commendations above many. He has the platform and way of conversion of the natives—and much studies the same—although he still lacks not opposition, as some others also have met with. But he will, without doubt, prove an instrument of much good in the country, being a good scholar and having skill in the tongues. He will prove that the way to instruct the Indians must be in their own language — not English — and that their language may be perfected.

★ ★ ★ ★ ★ ★ ★

AMERICA

by HENRY VAN DYKE
From *The White Bees and Other Poems*

Copyright, 1909, by CHARLES SCRIBNER'S SONS
Verses added in March, 1906, to the national hymn
written in 1831 by Reverend Samuel Francis Smith.

I love thine inland seas,
   Thy groves of giant trees,
   Thy rolling plains;
Thy rivers' mighty sweep,
Thy mystic canyons deep,
Thy mountains wild and steep,
   All thy domains;

Thy silver Eastern strands,
Thy Golden Gate that stands
   Wide to the West;
Thy flowery Southland fair,
Thy sweet and crystal air,—
O land beyond compare,
   Thee I love best!

★ ★ ★ ★ ★ ★ ★

An Account of a Voyage to America in About 1850

by J. Richard Beste

From *Adventures of an English Gentleman's
Family in the Interior of America*

Tor Bay—Torquay! what pleasant hours I had spent beside
that pretty shore! What hopes, what happiness, had sprung
to me from that calm retreat! And here we lie and look at it;
and the fishing boats supply us with fish; and the vessel sways
from side to side on the sunny waves for about eight and
forty hours. But then — up arose the breeze, and away we
went, westward! There was not much wind, but the effect
was disagreeable enough; and we had not much appetite when
we were called down to dinner.

"But what is this on the table?" I asked.

"A spider."

Dear landsman, I knew no more than you what "a spider"
meant on a dinner table on board ship: and I lifted up the
tablecloth to examine the wooden framework which covered
it all, and divided it into little boxes, about three inches deep
and twelve or more inches wide or long, according to the
size of the plates or dishes that were placed upon it. We all
admired the contrivance; and still more so when the ship leaned
on one side, and some plates, that had been set down at the
other end of the table beyond the "spider," slid upon the floor,
while our own dishes were firmly fixed in its fangs.

Captain Parsons had engaged to supply us with all proper
provisions as stateroom passengers; but he had so short a time
to lay in stores, that I was somewhat anxious as to how we
should fare. My wife had requested him to take on board a
goat to supply us with fresh milk, which we all found more
agreeable than the so-called preserved milk in tins. The preserved meats, however, which he took for us—the salmon, sar-
dines and tuna in oil—were excellent. Of poultry there was a
good store, though the ducks pined for want of water to swim
in. Fresh butcher's meat of course disappeared after the first
few days, and the eggs were no longer new laid: but the broiled
ham was plentiful and good; and by living very sparingly on
this, on curries, on preserved fish, with pickle and vinegar, I

managed to keep off all positive seasickness, and suffered only from the nasty nausea which I imagine to be inseparable from salt water. Then we had hot rolls, half baked according to the universal practice in America, and corn bread in abundance. This latter was not unpleasant, but too sweet for my palate. I was glad to see that my children liked it.

Our dinners were always at two o'clock: our breakfasts we persuaded our host to defer till near eight o'clock: and our teas were at seven. Fried and cold ham, and lots of omelets; with hot rolls and corn bread; with tea and coffee and fried potatoes, made these meals ample for those even of our party to whom the sea breeze gave most appetite. The Captain sat at the head of the table: his first mate next to our boys at the bottom; and as yet unused to the American plan of bolting their food, we marveled how the latter could get through his meals and be again on deck before we had well nigh begun ours. The Captain's evident wish to conform to our ways could not make even him sit what we thought a decent time at the board: and he always stole away on deck and smoked his one cigar after every meal before we were ready to rejoin him.

My poor wife, although the only one of the party who had been much at sea, and generally without sickness, suffered greatly on this voyage. She struggled against it at first, but then fairly gave in, and spent most of her mornings in her stateroom. The children, according to their different constitutions and the thoughtlessness or energy of their characters, suffered or escaped all ailing. The younger ones generally disregarded the nuisance: they ate, and were ill, and got well again, and played about and enjoyed the novelty of the scenes around them. Our invalid daughter suffered least from seasickness, and gained strength visibly in the fresh salt breeze. She was always up early on deck before breakfast, and soon acquired a tolerable footing on its heaving floor. She enjoyed carrying cups of tea or coffee to her mother's room, and showing that she could do so without spilling their contents, when, as she said, the ship "raised her bows to allow the wave to pass under her without splashing her face, or figurehead." Our eldest daughter looked after and tended all in their ailings and wants. Our little Isabel amused the youngest children, and constituted herself their day nurse. The one and the other were often sick, but silently rushed away and eased themselves, and then returned to their self-appointed duties with good nature and smiles as if nothing had happened. The boys ran wild, and pretended that they were learning navigation.

At nightfall, we all collected round the table in the saloon, and studied together the American books or atlases belonging to the Captain, in which, to our surprise, America was described first in endless district and county maps, while Europe was left to the end of the volume, and dismissed with scarcely one for each kingdom. We studied the maps, and fancied a home for our boys in the different states, and sketched and discussed plans of houses to be built for each, with one in the center of the location for us all to inhabit when we came to visit them, and which should always be transmitted to the head of the colony. Vain dreams, but pleasant!

*   *   *

A sea voyage is said to be tedious; but to a family afloat for the first time, it can never be without its excitement and incidents.

How interesting it was to hear captain and mate, with spy-glass in hand, speculate upon the identity of some vessel miles ahead—certain only that she was European because of the heaviness of her build and rigging — and break off the useless speculation, saying, "It matters not: we shall pass her shortly!" What pleasure it was then to feel that we were parties interested in the character of our pretty *Kate Hunter*, and to watch her stealing along the waters and gaining — gaining, till, in three hours, we passed the other, and recognized her as one that had left Le Hâvre a fortnight before ourselves!

How amusing it was to note the gambols of the dolphins which sometimes used to cover the sea like floating weeds—to mark them heaving their round glittering backs far above the blue wave, and then roll and tumble over as if they enjoyed the cool bathing and the power of swimming in it while the sun shone so bright overhead!

How exciting it was to be startled from our reading round the saloon lamp at night, by one of the boys, who had escaped on deck, rushing down and calling to us that the sea was on fire! Then how blissful to hang over the sides of the vessel and mark the bright phosphoric gleaming in the track of the rudder and around and on every side on the dark face of the ocean, whenever a tiny wave toppled over its surging crest, as if silver and gold sands were flashing up from beneath! The sky overhead was a deep dark blue, through which millions of stars brightly shone. A light wind was gently swelling out the white sail that hung from our tapering spars; and onwards, almost without motion, onwards glided our wedge-like clipper, as silent as the stars above or the ocean around; onwards into those bright phosphoric waves in front, and leaving a broad track of liquid flashes over the dark blue sea behind her.

And then, too, we had our broils and incidents of human life. Our German steward and the cook would often disagree; and once in their quarrels they issued forth where we could see them on the emigrant's deck; and the steward caught up a carving knife and was making towards his foe, when out rushed Captain Parsons, who seemed to be everywhere at once, and began silently to belabor the steward with a rope that he caught up. I promise you that the German bore on his person for many days the marks of that rope's-ending. Flogging is forbidden on board the merchant navy of the United States; but no captain hesitates to inflict it when he thinks necessary; and public opinion prevents the culprit from declaring his own ill conduct by informing against the lawbreaker.

One day, in crossing the deck, one of our emigrants fell and broke his leg. Captain Parsons was instantly there, and having caused the poor man to be laid upon a stretcher, he himself set the limb and bound it with splinters in a manner which, as I afterwards heard, was satisfactory to the surgeon on shore. We had no surgeon on board the *Kate Hunter*; and subsequent experience of him on the *Asia* steamer inclines me to exonerate those who chartered the vessel from the omission. Two poor little babies were born on board about this time; I know not if with our captain's assistance.

* * *

We had been becalmed several days since we started; and, on the 31st of May, being then one hundred and thirty miles from New York, were again lying idle, whistling for a wind. The captain and mate were very busy with their glasses; and, at length, distinguished a small open boat which had put off from the side of a vessel on the nature of which they had differed. This settled the question. By degrees, we were able to distinguish the six rowers who urged the little boat over the heaving sea; and after three hours' hard work, it came alongside of us and a pilot climbed on deck.

Few words were interchanged between him and the captain—men of business both; when the latter gave up the command of his vessel, and joyfully went down to his cabin to study the bundles of newpapers which had just been handed to him. But we were not yet at the end of our voyage. All that day, and the next, we lay becalmed with our pilot on board.

The next morning, I woke with a start, fearing that I had slept too long. It was four o'clock: and looking out of my little window, I saw the golden sun shining on land. It was a beautiful sight to one who had not seen land for three weeks. Long Island was on our right hand, and Staten Island, so I was told they were called, was on our left. Numbers of ships, boats, and steamboats of all kinds were on the water, which was beautifully blue, but not like the blue of the middle of the ocean.

Having left Le Hâvre in the afternoon of the 7th of May, and cast anchor in the night of the 1st and 2nd of June, we had made the voyage out in twenty-five days: not bad sailing, considering that we had been becalmed five or six.

A HOME SONG

by Henry van Dyke

From *The White Bees and Other Poems*
Copyright, 1909, by Charles Scribner's Sons

I read within a poet's book
    A word that starred the page:
"Stone walls do not a prison make,
    Nor iron bars a cage!"

Yes, that is true; and something more
    You'll find, where'er you roam,
That marble floors and gilded walls
    Can never make a home.

But every house where Love abides,
    And Friendship is a guest,
Is surely home, and home-sweet-home:
    For there the heart can rest.

On the Nature of Prudence

From *The Florentine Fior di Virtu of 1491*

Translated by Nicholas Fersin
Library of Congress catalogue card number: 53-60047

Prudence, or providence, according to Cicero, consists of three parts. The first is memory of things past. The second is intelligence, or capacity to discern that which one should do, truth from falsehood, good from evil, and to order all actions according to reason. The third part is providence, which is the preparing oneself beforehand according to one's needs. These two virtues take their source from other two virtuous traits: reason and solicitude. Aristotle says: "Reason is a certain discernment which takes us from one thing to the next in good order." Solicitude is a desire to do those things which one should do.

Example

The virtue of prudence, or providence, may be compared to the ant who is careful to find during the Summer all that it will need to nourish itself in wintertime. It remembers things past and recognizes the present, the Summer, as the time when it can gather all that it needs, thus providing for the future. The ant divides each grain it gathers into two parts so that it will not germinate during the Winter. It does all this following the advice, as it were, of a natural prudence or providence. Solomon, therefore, says: "Oh lazy & negligent one, go and learn from the ant who in the Summer gathers and stores all it will need in the Winter." Cicero says: "The wise man should never say, I did not think that such a thing could happen, because the wise man does not doubt, but hopes, does not sigh, but thinks." Solomon says: "Wisdom is better than all the wealth in the world. Whatever else thou couldst covet would never come close to wisdom." Jesus, son of Sirach, says: "Wine and grain gladden the hearts of men, but knowledge does so even more." And he also says: "Give liberally to the wise slave." And again: "Learn sciences and doctrines in thy youth and never stop until thy hair is white."

And he says: "All knowledge comes from God." David says: "Fear of God is the beginning of knowledge." Seneca says: "I would want to learn even if I had one foot in the grave." Ptolemy says: "The wise man can never die and he never feels pain. Really wise is the one who knows himself."

Persius says: "The heart of a wise & great man is like a ship: if it founders, many are drowned." Socrates says: "Science is written in the hearts of men and not on paper." Aristotle says: "The wise may combat any man simply by thinking." And he also says: "Insane is he who thinks that fortune brings good or evil. Knowledge brings good, madness brings evil." Branchus says: "The key to certainty is intensive thinking. We often err for not having thought enough." Alexander says: "Night was made to allow man to think about what he must do in the daytime."

Aristotle says: "Well pondered acts give sure clues of thinking intelligence." Seneca says: "It is easier to resist at the beginning of things than at the end." Eldecretus says: "He who starts wrongly cannot come to a good end." Martial says: "When grass is tender it may be pulled out easily, but when it sets its roots it may not be dug up without effort." Cato says: "Always think about and look at what may follow, for it is easy to combat an evil foreseen." Solomon says: "Go about your business with discernment and you will never be sorry." Pythagoras says: "No advice is better or more loyal than that given on a ship in danger." Socrates says: "He who listens to the advice of young people may well expect trouble." And he also says: "Three things are contrary to real discernment: haste, anger and greed." And he says: "To act slowly is a hateful thing, but it makes man wiser." Juvenal says: "Never reveal your intent to anyone of whom you wish to ask advice. Usually a man gladly tells another only that which he thinks may be well received. This is why tyrants may not last: no one ever tells them anything except what they want to hear." Seneca says: "If you want to ask advice of someone, first look to see how he acts himself." And he also says: "Thoughts are idly wasted where there is no advice, but where there are advisers the hearts of many men are reassured." Alexander says: "All things are made better by advice." Aristotle says: "Abstinence has made me chaste and study has made me ingenious." He also says: "Man should be diligent in taking advice and slow in giving it." Theophrastus says: "No good thing may last without solicitude." St. Sixtus says: "Running waters do not carry poison." Plato says: "Without experience and solicitude, knowledge is worth little."

Rules of Conversation

by WILLIAM PENN

Avoid *Company* where it is not *profitable* or necessary; and in those Occasions speak *little*, and *last*.

Silence is Wisdom, where Speaking is *Folly*; and always safe.

Some are so Foolish as to interrupt and anticipate those that speak, instead of hearing and thinking before they answer; which is uncivil as well as silly.

If thou thinkest twice before thou speakest once, *thou* wilt speak twice the better for it.

Better say nothing than not to the Purpose. And to speak pertinently, consider both what is fit, and when it is fit to speak.

In all Debates, let *Truth* be thy Aim, not Victory, or an unjust Interest: And endeavor to *gain*, rather than to expose thy Antagonist.

Give no Advantage in Argument, nor *lose* any that is offered. This is a Benefit which arises from *Temper*.

Don't use thy self to dispute *against* thine own Judgment, to show *Wit*, lest it prepare thee to be too *indifferent* about what is *Right*: nor against another Man, to *vex* him, or for mere Trial of Skill; since to *inform*, or to be *informed*, ought to be the *End* of all Conferences.

Men are too apt to be concerned for their *Credit*, more than for the Cause.

∽

Be not *easily* acquainted, lest finding Reason to cool, thou makest an *Enemy* instead of a good Neighbor.

Be Reserved, but not *Sour*; Grave, but not *Formal*; Bold, but not *Rash*; Humble, but not *Servile*; Patient, not *Insensible*; Constant, not *Obstinate*; Cheerful, not *Light*: Rather Sweet than *Familiar*; *Familiar*, than *Intimate;* and Intimate with *very few*, and upon *very good Grounds*.

Return the Civilities thou receivest, and be *ever* grateful for Favors.

Encouraging Idleness

Commentary by BENJAMIN FRANKLIN, circa 1750

I am one of that class of people, that feeds you all, and at present is abused by you all;—in short, I am a *farmer*.

By your newspapers we are told that God had sent a very short harvest to some other countries of Europe. I thought this might be in favor of Old England; and that now we should get a good price for our grain, which would bring millions among us, and make us flow in money: that to be sure is scarce enough.

But the wisdom of government forbade the exportation.

Well, says I, then we must be content with the market price at home.

No; say my lords the mob, you sha'nt have that. Bring your corn to market if you dare;—we'll sell it for you, for less money, or take it for nothing.

Being thus attacked by both ends *of the constitution*, the head and tail *of government*, what am I to do?

Must I keep my corn in the barn, to feed and increase the breed of rats?—be it so; they cannot be less thankful than those I have been used to feed.

Are we farmers the only people to be grudged the profits of our honest labor? And why? One of the late scribblers against us gives a bill of fare of the provisions at my daughter's wedding, and proclaims to all the world, that we had the insolence to eat beef and pudding! Has he not read the precept in the good book, *thou shalt not muzzle the mouth of the ox that treadeth out the corn*; or does he think us less worthy of good living than our oxen?

O, but the manufacturers! the manufacturers! they are to be favored, and they must have bread at a cheap rate!

Hark ye, Mr. Oaf:—The farmers live splendidly, you say. And pray, would you have them hoard the money they get? Their fine clothes and furniture, do they make them themselves, or for one another, and so keep the money among them? Or, do they employ these your darling manufacturers, and so scatter it again all over the nation?

The wool would produce me a better price, if it were permitted to go to foreign markets; but that, Messieurs the Public, your laws will not permit. It must be kept all at home, that our *dear* manufacturers may have it the cheaper. And then,

having yourselves thus lessened our encouragement for raising sheep, you curse us for the scarcity of mutton!

I have heard my grandfather say, that the farmers submitted to the prohibition on the exportation of wool, being made to expect and believe, that when the manufacturer bought his wool cheaper, they should also have their cloth cheaper. But the deuce a bit. It has been growing dearer and dearer from that day to this. How so? Why, truly, the cloth is exported: and that keeps up the price.

What is fair for one is fair for all

Now if it be a good principle, that the exportation of a commodity is to be restrained, that so our people at home may have it the cheaper; stick to that principle, and go thorough stitch with it. Prohibit the exportation of your cloth, your leather, and shoes, your iron-ware, and your manufactures of all sorts, to make them all cheaper at home. And cheap enough they will be, I will warrant you—till people leave off making them.

Some folks seem to think they ought never to be easy till England becomes another Lubberland, where it is fancied the streets are paved with penny-rolls, the houses tiled with pancakes, and chickens, ready roasted, cry, come eat me.

I say, when you are sure you have got a good principle, stick to it, and carry it through. I hear it is said, that though it was *necessary and right* for the ministry to advise a prohibition of the exportation of corn, yet it was *contrary to law;* and also, that though it was *contrary to law* for the mob to obstruct waggons, yet it was *necessary and right.* Just the same thing to a tittle. Now they tell me, an act of indemnity ought to pass in favor of the ministry, to secure them from the consequences of having acted illegally. If so, pass another in favor of the mob. Others say, some of the mob ought to be hanged, by way of example. . . . If so,— but I say no more than I have said before, *when you are sure that you have a good principle, go through with it.*

You say, poor laborers cannot afford to buy bread at a high price, unless they have higher wages. Possibly. But how shall we farmers be able to afford our laborers higher wages, if you will not allow us to get, when we might have it, a higher price for our corn?

By all that I can learn, we should at least have had a guinea a quarter more, if the exportation had been allowed. And this money England would have got from foreigners.

But, it seems, we farmers must take so much less, that the poor may have it so much cheaper.

A one-sided tax

This operates then as a tax for the maintenance of the poor. A very good thing, you will say. But I ask, why a partial tax? Why laid on us farmers only? If it be a good thing, pray, Messieurs the Public, take your share of it, by indemnifying us a little out of your public treasury. In doing a good thing, there is both honor and pleasure—you are welcome to your share of both.

For my own part, I am not so well satisfied of the goodness of this thing. I am for doing good to the poor, but I differ in opinion about the means. I think the best way of doing good to the poor, is, not making them easy *in* poverty, but leading or driving them *out* of it. In my youth I travelled much, and

I observed in different countries, that the more public provisions were made for the poor, the less they provided for themselves, and of course became poorer.

No country has provided more

And on the contrary, the less was done for them, the more they did for themselves, and became richer. There is no country in the world where so many provisions are established for them; so many hospitals to receive them when they are sick or lame, founded and maintained by voluntary charities; so many alms houses for the aged of both sexes, together with a solemn general law made by the rich to subject their estates to a heavy tax for the support of the poor. Under all these obligations, are our poor modest, humble, and thankful? And do they use their best endeavors to maintain themselves, and lighten our shoulders of this burthen?

Lack of incentive encourages idleness

On the contrary, I affirm, that there is no country in the world in which the poor are more idle, dissolute, drunken, and insolent. The day you passed that act, you took away from before their eyes the greatest of all inducements to industry, frugality, and sobriety, by giving them a dependence on somewhat else than a careful accumulation during youth and health, for support in age or sickness. In short, you offered a premium for the encouragement of idleness, and you should not now wonder, that it has had its effect in the increase of poverty. Repeal that law, and you will soon see a change in their manners; *Saint Monday*, and *Saint Tuesday*, will soon cease to be holidays. Six *days shalt thou labor*, though one of the old commandments long treated as out of date, will again be looked upon as a respectable precept; industry will increase, and with it plenty among the lower people; their circumstances will mend, and more will be done for their happiness by inuring them to provide for themselves, than could be done by dividing all your estates among them.

Excuse me, Messieurs the Public, if upon this *interesting* subject, I put you to the trouble of reading a little of *my* nonsense; I am sure I have lately read a great deal of *yours*, and therefore from you (at least from those of you who are writers) I deserve a little indulgence.

The American Flag

by Joseph Rodman Drake

From *American History by American Poets*
Edited by Nellie Urner Wallington
Copyright, 1911, by Duffield & Company

When Freedom from her mountain height
  Unfurled her standard to the air,
She tore the azure robe of night,
  And set the stars of glory there;
She mingled with its gorgeous dyes
The milky baldric of the skies,
And striped its pure, celestial white
With streakings of the morning light;
Then from his mansion in the sun
She called her eagle bearer down,
And gave into his mighty hand
The symbol of her chosen land.

★ ★ ★ ★ ★

Flag of the brave! thy folds shall fly,
The sign of hope and triumph high,
When speaks the signal trumpet tone,
And the long line comes gleaming on;
Ere yet the life-blood, warm and wet,
Has dimmed the glistening bayonet,
Each soldier eye shall brightly turn
To where the sky-born glories burn,
And, as his springing steps advance,
Catch war and vengeance from the glance,
And when the cannon-mouthings loud
Heave in wild wreaths the battle-shroud,
And gory sabres rise and fall,
Like shoots of flame on midnight's pall,
  Then shall thy meteor-glances glow,
And cowering foes shall sink beneath
  Each gallant arm that strikes below
That lovely messenger of death.

★ ★ ★ ★ ★

Flag of the free heart's hope and home,
  By angel hands to valour given;

Thy stars have lit the welkin dome,
  And all thy hues were born in heaven.
For ever float that standard sheet!
  Where breathes the foe but falls before us,
With Freedom's soil beneath our feet,
  And Freedom's banner streaming o'er us?

★ ★ ★ ★ ★

When the Great Gray Ships Come In

by Guy Wetmore Carryl

Ah, in the sweet hereafter Columbia still shall show
The sons of these who swept the seas how she bade them rise
    and go;
How, when the stirring summons smote on her children's ear,
South and North at the call stood forth, and the whole land
    answered "Here!"
For the soul of the soldier's story and the heart of the
    sailor's song
Are all of those who meet their foes as right should meet
    with wrong,
Who fight their guns till the foeman runs, and then, on the
    decks they trod,
Brave faces raise, and give the praise to the grace of their
    country's God!

Yes, it is good to battle, and good to be strong and free,
To carry the hearts of a people to the uttermost ends of sea,
To see the day steal up the bay, where the enemy lies in
    wait,
To run your ship to the harbor's lip and sink her across the
    strait:—
But better the golden evening when the ships round heads
    for home,
And the long gray miles slip swiftly past in a swirl of
    seething foam,
And the people wait at the haven's gate to greet the men
    who win!
Thank God for peace! Thank God for peace, when the
    great gray ships come in!

Census Taking at Sixty Dollars a Head

A story of Alaska's first census

From *Old Wagon Show Days* by Gil Robinson

Surrounded by a party of friends one evening, Bat Masterson held his listeners spellbound by reciting some stirring incidents in his career as a bad-man tamer in the Far West. While Masterson was going through the list of bad men from Ben Thompson, Doc Halliday, and the Earp Brothers to "Wild Bill" Hickok, the crowd was augmented by the arrival of Charlie Robinson, youngest son of John Robinson. Possibly there are very few of his friends who know of the fact that a little more than twenty-five years ago he was accounted one of the gamest men who ever left Seattle to invade the gold fields of Alaska. The Alaskan gold fever was upon the people, and Robinson decided to hunt fortune in that far away country, never for the moment anticipating that he would involuntarily be forced to assume the position of bad-man tamer when he reached the gold fields—unlike the men whom "Bat" talked about, nearly all of whom conducted their own graveyards in the West.

Charlie Robinson reigned as the terror of the bad men of Alaska for more than three years without a single notch in his gun-handle. He had a way of winning his battles without bringing the gun or bowie into play, and eventually news of his fearlessness reached the administration at Washington, and before he returned to the States he was selected by the Government to take part of the census of Alaska.

Mr. and Mrs. Robinson found themselves surrounded by a motley crowd when they boarded the steamer at Seattle that was to take them to Alaska. Mrs. Robinson was the only woman on the vessel, and it was not long before her husband discovered that he was going to face trouble in protecting his wife from insults of the big crowd which was made up of desperadoes and bad men from every section of the United States. The second day out he was forced to declare himself at the dinner table. One big bully named Dunston, hailing from the coal fields of Pennsylvania, and a desperado named Wilson, who had a reputation as a killer at his home in Wisconsin, engaged in obnoxious conversation at the table, and with his eyes flashing fire he warned them that anybody offering further insults would be answerable to him. Silence fell upon the diners and later when Robinson went out on deck he was followed by Dunston and Wilson.

"Pretty strong bluff you made in there, Robinson," said Wilson as he drew close to Robinson.

"I meant every word I said," replied Robinson, turning on the desperado from Wisconsin and looking him squarely in the face. His tone and manner evidently convinced Wilson that there was more than a bluff in Robinson's declaration and he retired to a corner of the vessel with Dunston and a number of other bad men to discuss the affair.

Disembarking at a point on the Yukon River, nearly all the passengers continued on the same trail and eventually brought up to a camp which they founded and christened Circle City. Here it was that the crude laws of a mining settlement were at once put in force and a vigilance committee was formed. Mr. Robinson was unanimously elected judge of the camp and in a brief speech he told the prospectors that he would administer justice in an impartial manner. Several shooting affrays occurred shortly after his induction into office, and the judge hunted up the principals and gave them a few hours to leave camp which they did. In the course of time a number of these desperados sneaked back into camp.

Judge Robinson realized that trouble was again brewing. He issued a call for a meeting of the vigilantes and it was decided to appoint a secret police force, the appointment of the members of which was left to the judge, realizing that the easiest way was the best. The judge did not make one appointment, but several days later he called the populace together and informed them that he had his secret police department, and insisted that everyone he had selected do his duty. The result was that every man in Circle City believed that the other fellow was a secret officer and peace reigned supreme for a long time and it was only the fear in which he was held by the would-be killers that saved his life.

After being unsuccessful in locating the yellow metal Mr. Robinson decided to return to Cincinnati, but the United States Government prevailed upon him to remain in Alaska and attempt the hazardous task of taking the census. Mr. Robinson would not agree to the request unless Mrs. Robinson be included in the proposition. It was finally decided to drop the bars, a woman census taker being an unlawful appointment. His wife was chosen as an assistant to her husband. Their salary was fixed by the Government at sixty dollars a day.

Mr. Robinson declared that he rode for days over the snow-covered ground without finding a white man or Indian to register. They traveled all over Alaska on a sledge drawn by six Alaskan dogs and at the conclusion of his work, which covered more than a year, Mr. Robinson handed in a census report which averaged a cost of sixty dollars each for every name obtained. With his brave little wife he faced death many times during the trip through the wilds of the gold-producing country. Battles with Indians who had never seen a white man were narrowly averted. Everywhere they found Indians, there was a scarcity of food and the cache that contained their edibles was invariably attacked by the redskins.

On one occasion all their food was stolen and they were left in a famished condition. Their hunger had become so intense that Mr. Robinson was on the point of killing one of the dogs, and was actually deliberating on which one of the faithful animals he would shoot, when a relief party came along and supplied them with food.

The Wayfarers

by RUPERT BROOKE

From *The Collected Poems of Rupert Brooke*
Copyright, 1915, by Dodd, Mead & Company
Copyright, 1943, by Edward Marsh

Is it the hour? We leave this resting-place
  Made fair by one another for a while.
Now, for a god-speed, one last mad embrace;
  The long road then, unlit by your faint smile.
Ah! the long road! and you so far away!
Oh, I'll remember! but . . . each crawling day
Will pale a little your scarlet lips, each mile
  Dull the dear pain of your remembered face.

. . . Do you think there's a far bordered town,
    somewhere,
  The desert's edge, last of the lands we know,
    Some gaunt eventual limit of our light,
  In which I'll find you waiting; and we'll go
Together, hand in hand again, out there,
  Into the waste we know not, into the night?

Mostly

for

Men

Some Observations on the Qualities Needed in Public Servants

by WILLIAM PENN

Y et the Public must and will be served; and they that do it well, deserve public Marks of Honor and Profit.

To do so, Men must have *public Minds*, as well as Salaries; or they will serve *private Ends* at the Public Cost.

Governments can never be well administered, but where those entrusted make *Conscience* of well discharging their Place.

Qualifications

Five Things are requisite to a good Officer; *Ability, Clean Hands, Dispatch, Patience and Impartiality.*

Capacity

He that understands not his Employment, whatever, else he knows, must be unfit for it, and the Public suffers by his Inexpertness.

They that are able, should be *just* too; or the Government may be *worse* for their Capacity.

Clean Hands

Covetousness in such Men prompts them to prostitute the Public for Gain.

The taking of a *Bribe* or *Gratuity*, should be punished with as severe Penalties, as the defrauding of the State.

Let Men have sufficient Salaries, and exceed them at their *Peril*.

It is a Dishonor to Government, that its Officers should live of Benevolence; as it ought to be Infamous for Officers to dishonor the Public, by being *twice* paid for the same Business.

But to be paid, and not to do Business, is *rank* Oppression.

A Tribute to His Country

by JOSEPH RUSSELL TAYLOR

From *Composition in Narration* by Joseph Russell Taylor
Published by Holt, Rinehart and Winston, Inc.

How should you answer if I should ask you—
What is the Nation? Where is it? Show it to me.
Does it look like the statue in New York Harbor?
Is it the fleet that recently went round the world,
with peaceful guns and with dancing on the decks?
Is it the flag, is it the capitol, has it the President's
many-caricatured countenance? Where and what
is the Nation? Is there such a thing?

You would answer that the Nation exists only in
the minds and hearts of men. It is an idea. It is therefore more real than its courts and armies; more real
than its cities, its railroads, its mines; its cattle; more
real than you and I are, for it existed in our fathers,
and will exist in our children. It is an idea, it is an
imagination, it is a spirit, it is human art. Who will
deny that the Nation lives?

Political Morality in the Mid-1800's

as observed by an English visitor

Preparations for the election had been going on with as much excitement and canvassing as could have occurred in England. Meetings were held almost every evening, and much eloquence was expended in fiery speeches. There was no treating or bribery, for as the votes were to be given by ballot, no prudent candidate would have spent money for what, after all, might be given against him without his knowledge: for the same reason, intimidation was out of the question, since none avowed their opinions but those who could afford to stand by them. As it was known that every man might speak for and promise one candidate and vote for another, promises and professions could have no other value than attached to the character of him who should make them. . . .

The bribed voter would have to be bribed upon a contingency: and these promises to pay upon a contingency would require so much honor in the briber and the bribee would be so open to discovery, and would be so much more costly than ready money, that the plan could never work.

It is a matter of fact that bribery and intimidation cannot take place where universal suffrage exists, as in America: let those who assert that it is impossible to prevent it with a limited constituency beware lest their arguments do not urge people to ask for universal suffrage, as being the lesser evil of the two.

With universal suffrage, it is impossible but that the universal will should be made apparent. I do not say here whether it is desirable that it should be so or not: I merely assert the fact.

Let it be understood that I am not arguing in favor of one system more than of another: I am merely stating what is the effect of the American plan. And here I assert the general feeling to be against bribery or intimidation. How or whence derived, I care not: but I do believe the general and individual feeling here to be so opposed to bribery and intimidation that a candidate or constituent, who should propose or submit to either, would find himself equally disgraced, not only in the public but in his own private estimation. A higher tone of political morality seems to preside at these than at our English elections.

Power and the Combative Instinct Grow As They Are Fed

Comments made by the press during the War of 1812
which are similar to those appearing in the news media of today

There are many evidences, however, that the intoxication of warlike expenditure is not to spend its force in simply making the nation's coasts and commerce safe; that the sense of power and the combative instinct grow as they are fed. There are in every country, our own being no exception, newspapers and public men who are always ready to float on the crest of a wave of popular passion, no matter whither it may be driving, or on what inhospitable shore it is to break in tumultuous surf at last.

The case will bring its peculiar temptations for the United States, for the navy is just that branch of the service for which our people have a traditional weakness, and on which they will spend the public money with least complaint. We may still echo the fine saying of Webster, in his appeal to Congress in 1814 for a naval rather than a land war: "Even our party divisions, acrimonious as they are, cease at the water's edge."

The dangers involved are of course too great to admit of parsimony. It was a pleasant jest of Washington's, when some one in the Convention of 1787 moved a permanent restriction of the standing army to 5000 men, to suggest as an amendment a solemn constitutional requirement that no enemy should ever invade the United States with more than 3000; and we should take care not to expose ourselves to the spirit of the sarcasm. But when the building of a single vessel has come to cost millions of dollars, instead of the modest two or three hundred thousand which sufficed to build even a 74-gun ship in 1815; when scores of ambitious naval officers are anxious to show a clear justification for this expenditure; and when the thoughtless people who are always ready to have every fancied insult wiped out in blood are the ones who are apt to be heard first, loudest, and most persistently, who shall say there is no possible danger in the "new navy?"

It is beyond question that it is a necessity; but in yielding for the time to the evident necessity it should be with the determination that the war-spirit shall find no further admission to the American policy than an honest, though liberal, estimate of the necessity of the case shall require.

The Spirit of America

Thoughts of Woodrow Wilson

What are the liberties of a people? I have often had an image of liberty in my mind—an illustration of it. You know that when a great engine runs free, as we say, its freedom consists in its perfect adjustment. All the parts are so assembled and united and accommodated that there is no friction, but a united power in all the parts. So I dream of political liberty when we understand one another, when we cooperate with one another, when we are united with one another—then we are free. And when the American people have thus joined together in a great enterprise of their common life they will wonder how it ever happened that they permitted that great special interest to grow up and overshadow and smother the growths in the garden; then they shall wonder it was ever necessary to summon them to the conclusions of the ballot.

Madison Square Garden, October 31, 1912

And my dream is this: that as the years go on and the world knows more and more of America, it will also drink at these fountains of youth and renewal, that it will also turn to America for those moral inspirations that lie at the base of human freedom, that it will never fear America unless it finds itself engaged in some enterprise inconsistent with the rights of humanity, and that America will come into the full light of that day when all shall know she puts human rights above all other rights, and that her flag is the flag not only of America, but the flag of humanity.

Fourth of July Celebration, Philadelphia, 1914

America did not come into existence to make one more great nation in the family of nations, to show its strength and to exercise its mastery. America opened her doors to everybody who wanted to be free and to have the same opportunity everybody else had to make the most of his faculties and his opportunities; and America will retain its greatness only so long as it retains and seeks to realize those ideals. No man ought to suffer injustice in America, no man ought, in America, to fail to see the dictates of humanity.

American Federation of Labor Building Dedication
Washington, D. C., July 6, 1914

Did you ever stop to reflect just what it is America stands for? If she stands for one thing more than another it is for the sovereignty of self-governing people, and her example, her assistance, her encouragement, have thrilled two continents in this Western world with all those fine impulses which have built up human liberty on both sides of the water. She stands, therefore, as an example of independence, as an example of free institutions, and as an example of disinterested international action in the maintenance of justice.

Why is it that every nation turns to us with the instinctive feeling that if anything touches humanity it touches us? Because it knows that ever since we were born as a nation we have undertaken to be the champions of humanity and the rights of men. Without that ideal there would be nothing that would distinguish America from her predecessors in the history of nations. Why is it that men that love liberty have crowded to these shores? Why is it that we greet them as they enter the great harbor at New York with that majestic Statue of Liberty holding up a torch whose visionary beams are supposed to spread abroad over the waters of the world and to say to all men, "Come to America where mankind is free, and where we love all the works of righteousness and of peace?"

Cleveland, January 29, 1916

The final test of the validity, the strength, the irresistible force of the American ideal has come. The rest of the world must be made to realize from this time on just what America stands for, and when that happy time comes when peace shall reign again and America shall take part in the undisturbed and unclouded counsels of the world, it will be realized that the promises of the fathers, the ambitions of the men who fought for the bloody soil of Kansas, the ideals of the men who thought nothing of their lives in comparison with their ideals, will have been vindicated and the world will say: "America promised to hold this light of liberty and right up for the guidance of our feet, and behold she has redeemed her promise. Her men, her leaders, her rank and file, are pure of heart; they have purged their hearts of selfish ambition and they have said to all mankind: 'Men and brethren, let us live together in righteousness and in the peace which springeth only from the soil of righteousness itself.'"

Kansas City, February 2, 1916

* * * * *

In Dispensing Justice,
Never Lose Sight of Mercy

Attributed to St. Ambrose in writing to a disciple

My dear Son, love your tears; do not put them off: in proportion as you have been prompt to the commission of a fault, be prompt to lament it. Let nothing make you careless under a sense of sin. If you are unable to avoid, at least restrain anger. Great glory is it to spare, where you have the power of inflicting an injury. Do not retaliate upon one who has sinned against you, according to his faults; knowing that judgment is coming upon yourself. Hate separates a man from the kingdom, withdraws him from heaven, casts him out of Paradise.

In all your actions imitate the good, emulate the holy. Have always before your eyes the examples of the saints. Keep company only with the good, since if you are a companion of their conversation, you will become also the companion of their virtue. It is hazardous to be associated with those whose lives are bad; better have their hate than their fellowship. An idle discourse quickly stains the thoughts; and what is willingly listened to, very readily passes into practice.

Let that only go from your lips which will carry no pollution to the ear. The mind is dependent upon the tongue; and is tried and proved by it; for out of the abundance of the heart the mouth speaketh. Withhold any word from utterance which edifies not the hearers; since he who represses not an idle word, is quickly drawn into mischief. Do not defile your own mouth with another's iniquity. Do not detract from one who has committed a fault, but give him counsel.

Correct your own life by observing the lives of others. Defend the life of no man by giving it a false color. Let neither stripes nor death itself terrify you, so long as your life is virtuous and pious. A curious spirit tends to hazardous presumption. Love rather to hear than speak; and to listen than talk. They are equally culpable who consent to evil, and commit evil; punishment will be the constant result of doing or acquiescing in wickedness. Whatsoever you do with sound discretion must be virtue; but virtue not accompanied with prudence is in the same estimation as vice.

Let your testimony injure no man. Let your conversation be irreprehensible, meriting the acceptance and commendation of all. Turn not aside from right judgment out of regard to any man, whether rich or poor. Look to the cause, and not the person. Distribute justice on a principle of proportionate retribution. He who pays regard only to present benefits has no prospect of future glory.

In dispensing justice never lose sight of mercy. That justice is impious which makes no allowance for human frailty. Do not despise any case coming before you for judgment, and condemn no one on arbitrary grounds of suspicion. Human judgment is always liable to deception.

Avoid honors which you cannot hold without blame. If honors exalt us, they make our crimes the greater. The higher our rank the more conspicuous is our delinquency; and the lower we are, the nearer are we to pardon. No one administers worldly affairs without sin. It is a wonder if a man abounding in wealth cultivates quiet. He who entangles himself in the things of earth separates himself from heaven. No man, at the same time, can cultivate God's favor and that of the world. It is hard to love both God and the world. Abstain from all commerce with him whom the world loves. Detach yourself from all business, as one dead to this world. As one buried to the world, have no care for it. While you are living, despise what after death you cannot retain.

Have compassion upon all, without distinction; for it is uncertain by compassionating whose case you may most please God. Take not from one to give to another; nor exercise compassion at another's expense. Such commiseration brings no credit with it, but rather condemns you.

The good you do, let it not be boastfully, but feelingly done; for if praise is your object, your reward is forfeited. Rewards are promised to the just, in heaven, not during their stay on earth.

Pay attention to whatever you read: and what you respect in reading, do not show contempt for by your mode of living.

* * * * *

No American who has caught the true historic enthusiasm of this great country that we love can be proud of it merely because of its accumulated great material wealth and power. The pride comes in when we conceive how that power ought to be used.

Woodrow Wilson
Jefferson Day Dinner, Washington, D. C.
April 13, 1916

Disappointments in Producing America's First Dictionary

A letter from Noah Webster to John Jay

Amherst, Mass., May 19, 1813

Sir,

Your favor of the 11th reached me last evening. You will perceive by the date of this that I am no longer an inhabitant of New Haven, nor of Connecticut.

In answer to your inquiry, I would inform you that there are subscription papers for my dictionary in New York, and one, I believe, in the hands of Whiting and Watson, but no attempts have been made for nearly two years to procure names.

Finding my own resources would not be adequate to the support of my family while I was engaged in the execution of the work, I made a serious effort to raise money by subscription, and an advance of part of the money. I visited New York, Philadelphia, Boston, Salem, Newburyport, etc. and laid before many principal literary gentlemen, not only my proposals, but a specimen of the work. I everywhere received assurances of liberal support, but on trial no names were procured except a few in New York and New Haven.

A year ago, my means failing, an attempt was made in New Haven, by some particular friends, to unite a few gentlemen in an undertaking to advance me a sum of money in three years which, with my own means, would probably enable me to carry my purpose into effect, and in fact, one third of the sum was advanced. I sat down at my studies for the year, supposing the other two thirds would be furnished in the two following years. At the end of the year, last spring, I was astonished to find that most of the gentlemen did not expect to make any further advances and I was suddenly left without the means of subsistence.

I had no alternative. I sold my house in New Haven at a loss, and purchased a house in Amherst whither I removed in September last. Here my expenses are less, and my family submits to new hardships, and a new mode of life with a good degree of fortitude. The details of facts are too numerous to be recited. I hope to be able to support my family here without farther aid; but this is by no means certain. I shall pursue my design, if kind providence shall permit. But the disappointments I have experienced, lead me to place no dependence on my fellow citizens. Some few of my friends would do all in their power to encourage me, but literary men in the large towns appear to be opposed to me or my design and their pointed opposition has had no small effect in preventing me from receiving encouragement.

If I live to finish my proposed work, it is probable I shall go to England to revise and publish it, and as my own country furnishes no patron, I may find one in Great Britain. I am so well satisfied that my researches will open an unexplored field and throw more light on the origin and history of language than all that has before been written as well as lead to important illustrations of ancient History, sacred and profane, that I think it my duty to pursue the subject, unless absolutely compelled to relinquish it.

I thank you, sir, for the interest you kindly manifest in my success, and am,

With great respect,
Your obedient servant,
Noah Webster

Through reading this simple comment by Webster, which was found among his memoirs, it is possible to imagine the thrill of finally completing the monumental task of building Webster's dictionary.

I finished writing my Dictionary in January, 1825, at my lodgings in Cambridge, England. When I had come to the last word, I was seized with a trembling which made it somewhat difficult to hold my pen steady for writing. The cause seems to have been the thought that I might not then live to finish the work, or the thought that I was so near the end of my labors. But I summoned strength to finish the last word, and then walking about the room a few minutes I recovered.

It is interesting to know that Webster himself performed the great manual as well as mental labor. The entire work — with all the authorities, quotations, and passages cited to illustrate the meaning of words — was written out in his own hand.

The Urgency of Better Education

by JOHN F. KENNEDY

For the nation, increasing the quality and availability of education is vital to both our national security and our domestic well-being. A free nation can rise no higher than the standard of excellence set in its schools and colleges. Ignorance and illiteracy, unskilled workers and school drop-outs—these and other failures of our educational system breed failures in our social and economic system: delinquency, unemployment, chronic dependence, a waste of human resources, a loss of productive power and purchasing power and an increase in tax-supported benefits. The loss of only one year's income due to unemployment is more than the total cost of twelve years of education through high school. Failure to improve educational performance is thus not only poor social policy, it is poor economics.

At the turn of the century, only 10 percent of our adults had a high school or college education. Today such an education has become a requirement for an increasing number of jobs. Yet nearly 40 percent of our youths are dropping out before graduating from high school; only 43 percent of our adults have completed high school; only 8 percent of our adults have completed college; and only 16 percent of our young people are presently completing college. As my Science Advisory Committee has reported, one of our most serious manpower shortages is the lack of Ph.D.'s in engineering, science and mathematics; only about one-half of one percent of our school-age generation is achieving Ph.D. degrees in all fields.

I do not say that the federal government should take over responsibility for education. That is neither desirable nor feasible. Instead, its participation should be selective, stimulative and, where possible, transitional.

A century of experience with land-grant colleges has demonstrated that federal financial participation can assist educational progress and growth without federal control. In the last decade, experience with the National Science Foundation, with the National Defense Education Act, and with programs for assisting federally affected school districts has demonstrated that federal support can benefit education without leading to federal control. The proper federal role is to identify national education goals and to help local, state and private authorities build the necessary roads to reach those goals. Federal aid will enable our schools, colleges and universities to be more stable financially and therefore more independent.

These goals include the following:

First, we must improve the quality of instruction provided in all of our schools and colleges. We must stimulate interest in learning in order to reduce the alarming number of students who now drop out of school or who do not continue into higher levels of education. This requires more and better teachers—teachers who can be attracted to and retained in schools and colleges only if pay levels reflect more adequately the value of the services they render. It also requires that our teachers and instructors be equipped with the best possible teaching materials and curricula. They must have at their command methods of instruction proven by thorough scientific research into the learning process and by careful experimentation.

Second, our educational system faces a major problem of quantity—of coping with the needs of our expanding population and of the rising educational expectations for our children which all of us share as parents. Nearly 50 million people were enrolled in our schools and colleges in 1962—an increase of more than 50 percent since 1950. By 1970, college enrollment will nearly double, and secondary schools will increase enrollment by 50 percent—categories in which the cost of education, including facilities, is several times higher than in elementary schools.

Third, we must give special attention to increasing the opportunities and incentives for all Americans to develop their talents to the utmost—to complete their education and to continue their self-development throughout life. This means preventing school drop-outs, improving and expanding special educational services, and providing better education in slum, distressed and rural areas where the educational attainment of students is far below par. It means increased opportunities for those students both willing and intellectually able to advance their education at the college and graduate levels. It means increased attention to vocational and technical education, which have long been underdeveloped in both effectiveness and scope, to the detriment of our workers and our technological progress.

In support of these three basic goals, I am proposing today a comprehensive, balanced program to enlarge the federal government's investment in the education of its citizens—a program aimed at increasing the educational opportunities of potentially every American citizen, regardless of age, race, religion, income and educational achievement.

Special Message to Congress
Washington, D. C.
January 29, 1963

You Do Not Pick Friends As
You Do a Wife

The nature of matrimony is one thing, and the nature of friendship is another.

A tall man likes a short wife.

A great talker likes a silent woman—for both can't talk at once.

A gay man likes a domestic gal—for he can leave her at home with the children while he is enjoying himself at parties.

A man that has no music in him likes it in his spouse—and so on.

It chimes beautifully for they aren't in each other's way.

* * * * *

Now friendship is the other way. You must like the same things—have a similarity of tastes, studies, pursuits, and recreations—to like each other and be friends, or what they call congenial souls.

A toper for a toper.

A smoker for a smoker.

A horse-racer for a horse-racer.

A prize-fighter for a prize-fighter—and so on.

Matrimony likes contrasts; friendship seeks its own counterparts.

SOLITUDE

by Lewis Carroll

I love the stillness of the wood:
  I love the music of the rill:
I love to couch in pensive mood
  Upon some silent hill.

Scarce heard, beneath yon arching trees,
  The silver-crested ripples pass;
And, like a mimic brook, the breeze
  Whispers among the grass.

Here from the world I win release,
　　Nor scorn of men, nor footstep rude,
Break in to mar the holy peace
　　Of this great solitude.

Here may the silent tears I weep
　　Lull the vexed spirit into rest,
As infants sob themselves to sleep
　　Upon a mother's breast.

But when the bitter hour is gone,
　　And the keen throbbing pangs are still,
Oh, sweetest then to couch alone
　　Upon some silent hill!

To live in joys that once have been,
　　To put the cold world out of sight,
And deck life's drear and barren scene
　　With hues of rainbow-light.

For what to man the gift of breath,
　　If sorrow be his lot below;
If all the day that ends in death
　　Be dark with clouds of woe?

Shall the poor transport of an hour
　　Repay long years of sore distress —
The fragrance of a lonely flower
　　Make glad the wilderness?

Ye golden hours of Life's young spring,
　　Of innocence, of love and truth!
Bright, beyond all imagining,
　　Thou fairy-dream of youth!

I'd give all wealth that years have piled,
　　The slow result of Life's decay,
To be once more a little child
　　For one bright summer-day.

Those Who Encourage Anarchy at Home Join Hands with Our Enemies Abroad

A statement by Theodore Roosevelt in 1899

Are the people of this country so short-sighted that they forget the miseries of six years ago? Do they forget the bread riots, the poverty, the squalid want, even of those able and anxious to work? I appeal to the evidence of your own senses. Are you or are you not better off than you were six years ago? The farmer, the tradesman, the man with the dinner pail, the wage-worker—are these men as a whole better or worse off than they were six years ago?

In a great community there is, and there always will be, individual suffering, not only among the shiftless and the ne'er-do-wells, but at certain times and in certain places among the honest and industrious with whom fate has gone hard. We cannot by any laws bring happiness and prosperity to everyone, but we can do what the Republican party has actually done; that is, by wise legislation and wise administration secured the chance for the great bulk of our people to live out their lives and do their work with the odds as much as possible in their favor; the conditions as favorable as they can be made.

In the long run it is not in the power of any man or of any outside force to lower the standard of living of the American workingman, unless the American workingman does it himself. If the wage-workers act with wisdom and with forethought, if they show far-sighted prudence in their combinations, industrial and political, their ultimate welfare is assured. In the long run only the American workingman can hurt himself.

* * * * *

Those who would encourage anarchy at home must naturally strike [join] hands with the enemies of our country abroad. The friend of the bomb-thrower and his apologists are doing what is fit and meet when they strike hands across the seas with those who are fighting our soldiers in foreign lands. Fundamentally the causes which they champion are the same. The step from encouraging the assassination of the guardians of the law at home to the aiding and abetting of the shooting down of our soldiers abroad is but a short one; and it matters little whether the encouragement be given by the exercise of the pardoning power, by raving speeches upon the platform, or by the circulation of silly documents composed by men too feeble to accomplish the mischief they design.

Make no mistake! In the Philippines we are at war with an enemy who must be put down. It is absolutely impossible to save our honor except through victory, and it is equally impossible to win peace, to restore order in the islands, or to prepare the way for self-government there save through victory. Every argument that our opponents make now is exactly such as if they were logical they would make on behalf of the Sioux Indians in South Dakota or the Apaches in New Mexico, and such as they actually did make at the outbreak of the Civil War. If we have no moral right to interfere in the Philippines then we have no moral right to interfere in an Indian reservation. If we have no right in Luzon and should leave it to the Tagals, then we have no right in Alaska and should leave it to the Indians and Eskimos. Not one argument can be made for the proposed line of conduct in the one case that does not apply with exactly as much force to the other.

In Memory of My Father
by GELETT BURGESS

My father died when I was all too young,
And he too old, too crowded with his care
For me to know he knew my hot, fierce hopes,—
Youth sees wide chasms between itself and Age —
How could I think he, too, had lived my life?
My dreams were all of war, and his, of rest.

And so he sleeps (please God), at last at rest,
And it may be, with soul refreshed, more young
Than when he left me, for that other life —
Free, for a while at least, from that old Care
The hard relentless torturer of his Age
That cooled his youth, and bridled all his hopes.

For now I know he had the longing hopes,
The wild desires of youth, and all the rest
Of my ambitions, ere he came to Age,
He too was bold, when he was free and young —
Had I but known that he could feel, and care!
How could I know the secret of his life?

In my own youth I see his early life
So reckless, and so full of buoyant hopes.
I see him jubilant, without a care,
The days too short, and grudging time for rest —
He knew the wild delight of being young, —
Shall I too know the calmer joys of Age?

His words come back, to mind me of that age
When lovingly he watched my broadening life, —
And, dreaming of the days when he was young
Smiled at my joys, and shared my fears and hopes.
His words still live, for in my heart they rest,
Too few, not to be kept with jealous care!

Ah, little did I know how he could care!
That in my youth lay joys to comfort Age!
Not in this world, for him, was granted rest,
But, as he lived in me, a happier life,
He prayed more earnestly, to win my hopes,
Than ever for his own, when he was young!

He once was young; I too must fight with Care;
He knew my hopes, and I must share his Age;
God grant my life be worthy, too, of Rest!

Dempsey versus Carpentier

A ringside report of a fight occurring nearly a half-century ago which is still exciting copy

From *Spink Sport Stories* by AL SPINK
Copyright 1921 by The Spink Sport Stories Co.

Tex Rickard guaranteed Carpentier $200,000 for his share, win, lose or draw, while Dempsey was guaranteed $300,000, win, lose or draw.

Rickard, great sportsman that he is, handled the big match all alone and for his nerve and sportsmanship got in a gate that ran to the $1,600,000 mark.

Just before the fight both Dempsey and Carpentier issued last minute statements, asserting they were ready for the battle of their lives, and breathing confidence in the outcome.

Odds favoring the champion had shortened markedly in the last hours of betting, but Dempsey still reigned a 2 or 2½ to 1 favorite over the French challenger. Carpentier, however, ruled the sentimental favorite.

New York newspapers, whose accounts of the coming fight were measured by pages rather than columns, were a study in superlatives.

The fight was described as the "greatest heavyweight encounter in the history of sport." It was staged in the "biggest arena ever constructed" before the "largest and most brilliant assembly ever turned out for a sporting event," and the purse—$500,000—was "the most generous in the history of the ring."

Dempsey was described as "the greatest heavyweight champion since John L. Sullivan," while the handsome Frenchman was called a "Greek god, mystery man, man of destiny" and "wonder man," and acclaimed as the "greatest heavyweight Europe ever produced."

The bout unquestionably excited the greatest interest ever aroused by a pugilistic encounter. The crowd that was struggling its way out toward Boyle's Thirty Acres in Jersey City all through the forenoon of July 2 assembled from every corner of the world. Representative citizens from far west, middle west, south and east had been rolling into the city for forty-eight hours on every train, while steamers deposited hundreds of enthusiasts from France, England, Spain—even from faraway Japan and China.

Among the spectators were prominent state and city officials, an assistant secretary of the navy, scientists, artists, theatrical stars and impresarios, men whose names are famous in every field of sport, and just plain citizens. It was estimated that at least 5,000 women and 90,000 men were in the big arena when the gong for the main bout rang at 3 o'clock.

The Fight by Rounds

First round — When the bell starting the first round sounded, the Frenchman leaped like a tiger at the American, his left fist crunched against Jack's chin and he clinched. Dempsey began pecking at his body. Carpentier broke and leaped back, only to spring back again with a terrific right-hander that caught Dempsey high on the side of the head. To the amazement of the crowd, Carpentier was forcing the fight, but Dempsey was not to be driven back. He lowered his head and came grimly in, his blows driving home at short range; and at times he shot his clenched fists through small openings into the Frenchman's body.

This was his plan of battle—to wear Carpentier down. In the middle of the round Carpentier drove a right squarely against Dempsey's chin. The blow would have knocked out any but a man of iron.

Dempsey's knees shook and his face turned gray. He looked sick and dazed. For a moment even the grim determination was wiped from his face. Another blow and he would go down, but even as Carpentier drew back his hand Dempsey recovered and lunged foward, smashing at Carpentier's body so hard that Georges was forced to give ground before the attack.

Now came blow on blow, so fast the eye could hardly follow. Carpentier's lefts and rights shot home, and Dempsey clouted grimly in return. Once, Georges, who seemed to put every ounce of his strength into one crashing blow when he saw a sure opening, swung so furiously at Dempsey's chin that, merely grazing it, he whirled and fell headlong through the ropes.

Ertle jumped forward, but Dempsey, a sportsman, had already started back to let his opponent come back. Carpentier slipped off the ropes and started after Dempsey again. His blue eyes were full of battle, his smooth brow corrugated — you

could see him think. Circling, he attacked again, and this time
his flashing right fist reached Dempsey's chin and shook him.
Dempsey pushed in, still grim, and forced Georges to retreat
and the bell rang.

The crowd buzzed with excitement during the minute of
rest. There was no doubt about it—Carpentier was as adver-
tised; this was to be no cinch for the champion.

Second round—Carpentier came out for the second round
to attack again. His face was a mask of concentration, through
which glimmered now and then a slight cynical smile. He
studied Dempsey. Blows were exchanged, with little advantage, and it went along to the middle of the round.

And then, as if he had been saving himself for a supreme effort, he leaped in and drove a crashing right-hander to

Dempsey's jaw. Before Dempsey could recover Carpentier had struck again and again and still again, all right-hand blows, with furious speed and strength behind them.

Dempsey reeled back, his knees bent and his legs shaking. He was staggering. He wavered to one side a little before he could turn to meet his man, and again Carpentier clouted him on the chin.

Dempsey made a few quick little steps and, like a bluff-bowed ship beating offshore against a heavy sea, went lurching ahead. He was dazed but grimmer, more doggedly determined for the beating that came to him.

In that moment there was no doubt that Jack Dempsey was a champion, no doubt that he could take punishment and fight, for Carpentier had hit him harder than any man ever hit him before and he was weathering it. Carpentier tried another rally, and Jack met him, swinging blow for blow. For once Dempsey was wild. His fist hit nothing but the empty air as the Frenchman changed his plan for a moment and slipped deftly out of danger. The second was Carpentier's round—but it was still anybody's fight. As Dempsey went to his corner his seconds worked on him furiously, and Jack Kearns, his veneer of calmness gone, put a trembling hand on the ropes and leaned over to give hurried instructions.

Carpentier in his corner, looking anxiously across the ring, had a red lump under his left eye and his nose was slightly cut. Dempsey was still unmarked.

Third round—The third started like another whirlwind. Dempsey went straight across the ring, but Carpentier slipped deftly away and ducked under a blow that might have dropped him. He was studying Dempsey again, watching keenly for an opening, intent on holding his advantage and taking less risk of being stopped by Dempsey's slashing blows.

Dempsey held his hands high, just under his chin, as if to guard against the right-hand blows that had dazed him before.

Carpentier missed two or three times, and as they came into close quarters he suddenly shifted his attack and drove two terrific right-hand uppercuts beneath Dempsey's high guard, landing fairly on his chin. His cold blue eyes were alert, his lips drawn in a slight smile as he watched Dempsey's face to see how much he was hurting him.

Apparently he felt himself master of the situation, but he was making no mistakes. The championship was within reach of his hand, but there was the fast, hard fighting Dempsey pressing in, driving spiteful punches to the Frenchman's body whenever they came to grips, so he was wary.

Carpentier outboxed him, moved swiftly, leaped in high on his toes to attack, leaped away to safety. But the Frenchman was weakening. His speed came in spasmodic spurts—amazing speed and power, but not continuous like Dempsey's attack. Just before the end of the round the champion drove a terrible right-hand blow into Carpentier's body. Carpentier clung tightly in a clinch. He was weak. But it was still anybody's fight when the bell rang.

Fourth and last round — Now in the fourth, Dempsey drew on his reservoir of strength and pressed Carpentier hard. The French boy was shifty, foxy, alert. He leaped into attack and his quick blows struck home, but they seemed to lack the crushing force of the round before.

The body hammering was bringing him down. Carpentier hit Dempsey on the chin, left and right, and Dempsey retaliated with a right, a crushing body blow fairly in the pit of the stomach and near the heart. Before Carpentier could move, a short left hook struck him on the chin, and he went down heavily on his face. The crowd leaped up, a roar went from ringside to the fluttering American and French flags in the distance.

Dempsey walked back to his corner. Carpentier pulled his legs up a little and lay there motionless. Ertle tolled off the seconds—up to nine—and at the sound the game Frenchman leaped from flat on his stomach to his feet, whirled, and waited for Dempsey to come at him.

Carpentier was in sad condition then. He was dazed and weak, but he slipped aside a little to evade Dempsey's first rush, and faced his man with gleaming eyes and a smile on his lips.

Dempsey closed in deliberately. There was a little swirling scrimmage and out of it shot Carpentier in a headlong plunge, dropped by Dempsey's short right-hand blow to the chin. Dempsey walked away, and the French boy rolled to his side, lifted his leg and tried with all his might to come up again. His eyes shut and his forehead creased with effort.

He raised a little as the count went on, but fell back helpless when Ertle reached ten. Then, and only then, Deschamps leaped into the ring, his face twisted as with pain, and lifted the fallen champion of Europe from the ground.

Other willing hands seized him and dragged him to his corner. Dempsey had turned to wave to Kearns that it was all over. He turned again and walking swiftly to Carpentier's corner seized the still dazed Frenchman by the hand.

"Too bad, Georges," Dempsey said. "You made a great fight."

Carpentier looked up and smiled. Some sportsman, that French boy—and some sportsman, Jack.

Before Dempsey left the ring Referee Ertle removed his gloves, inspected his bandages again and found them all right.

*   *   *

Carpentier broke his right thumb in two places and suffered a bad wrist sprain in the second round of the fight. This was reported by Dr. Joseph Connolly of Glen Cove, N. Y., who examined him at his training camp after the fight.

Carpentier's other external injuries were a slight cut under the left eye and a swollen nose.

Pierre Mallet, friend and adviser, said that Georges received the injury to his thumb eight days before while working with a sparring partner. His manager did not care to say anything about it at the time, as he felt the announcement might be taken as preparing the ground work for an excuse.

When told that Carpentier had broken a thumb, Jack Dempsey said he had not heard of it.

"If that is so, I am very sorry it happened," he said.

Not from the grand old masters,
  Not from the bards sublime,
Whose distant footsteps echo
  Through the corridors of Time.

For, like strains of martial music,
  Their mighty thoughts suggest
Life's endless toil and endeavor;
  And to-night I long for rest.

HENRY WADSWORTH LONGFELLOW